All of God's Word is food for our souls and Dr. Davis is not afraid to give it to us. In *My Exceeding Joy*, this beloved expositor continues to show us in the Psalms how the Word is made fresh through the work and personality of an unashamed and approved workman.

BRENT SADLER
Army Chaplain, 7th Special Forces Group, Florida

Dale Ralph Davis belongs to the rarest tribe of commentators: clearly communicating biblical truth with simultaneous theological depth and engaging devotional impact. The genuine love for Yahweh which oozes from these pages—not overly demonstrative but irresistibly contagious—enables readers to share both that same love and the 'Exceeding Joy' it produces.

MIKE BIGGS
Senior Pastor, Christ the King Presbyterian Church,
Norman, Oklahoma

Dale Ralph Davis has become the friend we all want by our side when reading the Bible. He is always a few steps ahead, clearing the path and lighting the way, and as we follow we find treasures we would have missed without his aid. This expository pilgrimage through the Psalms continues to delight, instruct, refresh and nourish our hearts. Above all else, Dr. Davis's own delight in God, evident on every page, leads us to his altar and displays his love and glory in ways that make us stop and pray and praise.

DAVID GIBSON
Minister, Trinity Church, Aberdeen, Scotland

T0001164

MY
EXCEEDING
JOY

An Exposition of Psalms 38–51

Dale Ralph Davis

CHRISTIAN
FOCUS

Copyright © Dale Ralph Davis 2023

paperback ISBN 978-1-5271-1068-7
ebook ISBN 978-1-5271-1112-7

10 9 8 7 6 5 4 3 2 1

Published in 2023
by
Christian Focus Publications Ltd.,
Geanies House, Fearn, Ross-shire,
IV20 1TW, Scotland, Great Britain

www.christianfocus.com

Cover design by
Daniel Van Straaten

Printed by Bell & Bain, Glasgow

CONTENTS

Abbreviations

ABD	*Anchor Bible Dictionary*
AV/KJV	Authorized/King James Version
EBC	*Expositor's Bible Commentary*
ESV	English Standard Version
GW	God's Word (World Publishing, 1995)
JB	The Jerusalem Bible (1966)
LXX	The Septuagint
NASB	New American Standard Bible
NBD	*New Bible Dictionary*, 3rd ed. (1996)
NEB	New English Bible
NET	NET Bible, New English Translation
NIDOTTE	*New International Dictionary of Old Testament Theology and Exegesis*
NIB	*New Interpreter's Bible*
NIV	New International Version
NKJV	New King James Version
NJB	New Jerusalem Bible (1985)
NJPS	Tanakh: A New Translation of the Holy Scriptures according to the Traditional Hebrew Text (1985)
NRSV	New Revised Standard Version
REB	Revised English Bible
RSV	Revised Standard Version
TEV	Today's English Version
TOTC	*Tyndale Old Testament Commentaries*
TWOT	*Theological Wordbook of the Old Testament*

PREFACE

There's such a variety in any chunk of the Psalms one selects to study. Psalms 38–51 stand as a case in point. Not that there's not a certain shape to the whole book of Psalms but there's still a certain 'messiness' in their appearance (cf. Eugene Peterson, *Answering God*, 107). They are not collected together into strict topical categories, which makes for a problem if one wants to select a title for a whole batch of them (like 38–51), because whatever title one selects won't 'fit' any number of those psalms. But that doesn't matter; it simply means I can select whatever title I want. And I have always been aghast (in a good sense) at the way the psalmist speaks of God in Psalm 43:4, when he writes of going to God 'my exceeding joy.' Isn't that thrilling? Do we usually think of the living God that way? I fear I do not, but I want to think of Him that way, though my spiritual anemia erodes that desire. But that doesn't keep me from loving the appeal of that text. So I've sort of wanted to write a book that carries that title. So … that is the title of this book. I can do this because I'm writing the book.

Housekeeping Matters

The translations are my own unless marked otherwise. For the personal, covenant name of God I use 'Yahweh' rather than 'the LORD.' 'Yahweh' is a personal name, 'the LORD' is a title. I have a wife, but I don't call her 'the wife'; I call her by her first name. Hence my preference for 'Yahweh,' though less familiar to many Bible readers.

I have two sisters-in-law named Joan. They have both known much joy, I think, that has yet been mixed, I know, with sorrow, loss, disappointment, and pain. And in it all, they go on believing in Jesus. This book is sent out as a small appreciation to the 'double Joans' for the encouragement that leaks over into our own faith from their discipleship.

DALE RALPH DAVIS

Psalm 38

A psalm. David's. To bring to remembrance.

(1) Yahweh, don't rebuke me in your wrath, and don't
  chasten me in your fury,

(2) for your arrows have sunk into me, and your hand has
  sunk down upon me.

(3) There is no sound place in my flesh
    because of your rage;
  there is no wholeness in my bones
    because of my sin.

(4) For my iniquities have gone over my head,
  like a heavy burden their weight is more than I can handle.

(5) My wounds reek, they ooze,
    because of my folly.

(6) I am terribly bent down, laid out;
  all day long I go around mourning,

(7) for my sides are filled with burning,
  and there is no sound place in my flesh.

(8) I've become numb and I've been terribly crushed;
    I roar because of the groaning of my heart.

(9) Lord, all my desire is before you,
  and my sighing has not been hidden from you.

(10) My heart hammers, my strength forsakes me,
and the light of my eyes—even that has gone from me.

(11) My friends and my companions stand off from my plague,
and those near me stand a long ways away.

(12) And those seeking my life set traps,
and those seeking to harm me have spoken ruin
—and all day long they keep mulling over deceits.

(13) But I am like a deaf fellow—I don't hear,
and (I'm) like a dumb person who doesn't open his mouth.

(14) So I became like a man who doesn't hear
and like one with no rebukes in his mouth.

(15) Because for **you**, Yahweh, I have waited;
you will answer, O Lord, my God.

(16) For I said, 'Lest they rejoice about me'
—when my foot slips they boast themselves against me.

(17) Indeed, I am ready to fall
and my pain is continually before me.

(18) Yes, I declare my iniquity,
I am distressed because of my sin.

(19) And my enemies, how alive! They are strong,
and those who hate me wrongly have multiplied

(20) and pay back evil for good
—they oppose me for pursuing good.

(21) Don't forsake me, Yahweh;
O my God, don't be far from me.

(22) Hurry to help me,
O Lord, my salvation.

1
When Trouble Is 'Complicated-er'...

Some time ago, *World* magazine told of an Indiana teenager who lost control of her car, rammed into a hollow tree, and suffered broken legs. That was the simple part. Seems when she hit the tree she smashed the home of some honeybees, who apparently were moved to intense anger. The bees plagued the attempts of paramedics and firefighters to free the girl. So a paramedic and seven firefighters accompanied the girl to the hospital where they were all treated for scores of bee stings. Somehow it couldn't be a normal road accident—it had to be complicated by all these additional hazards.

Which is a bit like Psalm 38. It's sometimes dubbed a 'penitential' psalm because it features confession for sin, but there is far more than that in it. The heading says it is meant 'to bring to remembrance.' That may mean it was to be used in conjunction with a memorial sacrifice or it may simply mean it was meant to remind the psalmist of the whole experience. The psalm falls into two major sections (vv. 1-14, vv. 15-22), which we consider in turn.

First, in verses 1-14, we meet with **an extensive description of a complex trouble**. As we stick our noses in the text, we find he is troubled over his *guilt* (vv. 1-4). He fears Yahweh's wrath and fury (v. 1), which, along with his sin, has had adverse physical effects (no 'sound place in my flesh,' 'no wholeness in my bones,' v. 3). He is overwhelmed and crushed by the weight of his iniquities. It's as if Yahweh's arrows have nailed him (v. 2a). Allen Ross notes that the psalm nowhere specifies what the sin is or sins are. We have no need to know that. But clearly conscious sin and chastening wrath are at the root of his trouble.

This sin-plus-chastisement seems to involve *disease* or illness of some sort (vv. 5-7). His wounds reek and ooze (v. 5), his sides burn (v. 7); again (see v. 3) he says there is 'no sound place in my flesh' (v. 7b). It seems like his guilt has brought about some severe physical and loathsome symptoms. Verse 8, which mentions his roaring, suggests the helpless *frustration* he feels in the midst of it all. The guilt on his conscience (vv. 1-4) and the ravages of illness or disease (vv. 5-7) have, not surprisingly, brought on *exhaustion* (v. 10); and his physical demise ensures his *isolation* (v. 11)—former friends and associates are not enamored to spend time with gross and loathsome cases (v. 5). All of which brings about extreme *peril* (v. 12), for it's clear that someone in his condition is nothing but vulnerable to schemes and attacks. It all seems to reduce him to a state of *indifference* (vv. 13-14); he might just as well play deaf and dumb to it all; apathy seems the name of the game. If you look carefully at these seven marks of

David's condition, maybe you can sense how multi-faceted a believer's conflicts and troubles can be. We prefer simple troubles if we must have them; but sometimes, as in Psalm 38, they are a twisted, complicated mess. Here is a spiritual, physical, psychological, social, hostile quagmire.

How should we react to this plot of text? Hopefully, by recognizing how very complex and complicated the troubles of God's people often are. We love to simplify, because then we can better control. But sometimes, the dilemmas of the saints are not like that at all.

During the eleven months Luther spent in Wartburg castle, after his 'kidnapping,' conditions in Wittenberg deteriorated. Under the preaching of Carlstadt and others, violence and mobs seemed the order of the day, which imposed a sort of Reformation-by-force. It was near thuggery—smashing altars, shrines, stained-glass windows, and insulting people who wanted to stay loyal to Roman Catholicism. So the town magistrates appealed to Luther to return. He did. And with his preaching brought calm. He insisted that their chaos was not gospel-produced reformation. Among other things he told them:

> Give people time! It took me three years of constant study, reflection, and discussion to arrive where I am now. Can the ordinary man, who has no education in such matters, be expected to move the same distance in three months?[1]

He was simply saying that 'It's not as simple as you're making it; people have to process these things; they have to think them through, need to be patiently taught,

1   N. R. Needham, *2000 Years of Christ's Power*, 5 vols. (Ross-shire: Christian Focus Publications, 2004), 3:131.

have such matters explained.' That's the way it is with the troubles of the Lord's people—they can be terribly complex and twisted and involved, and we must beware of whipping out some knee-jerk solution for them just because it sounds like good bumper-sticker theology.

That is one matter. Note again that I've called this section 'an *extensive description* of a complex trouble.' After all, he goes on for 14 verses. David goes into every nook and cranny of his difficulty, revealing his assumption that *God has the time* for all of this. What a marvelous God David has! Spurgeon once wrote, 'We are in such a hurry with poor troubled spirits that we hasten them on to the end of the sentence, and try to make them skip the weary details.' He told of a fellow gospel minister who called on one of his poor people, a lady who told him how much she'd enjoyed his call. He had scarcely said a word to her and yet she had told him he had done her much good. So, candid fellow that he was, he asked her how it could be—how could he have done her good when he'd hardly said a word? Her response: 'Ah, sir, you have listened so kindly: you have heard all I had to say, and there are very few who will do that.'[2] That is the God David has—a God who is willing to hear all 'the dreary details.'

But, of course, David knows Yahweh already knows all these details. That's clear in that little verse hidden away in the middle of all this, verse 9:

> Lord, all my desire is before you,
> and my sighing has not been hidden from you.

---

2   L. A. Banks, ed., *Spurgeon's Illustrative Anecdotes* (New York: Funk & Wagnalls, 1906), pp. 196-97.

He knows the Lord is completely aware of what he wants. As Kidner implies, the text is akin to Matthew 6:8, 'For your Father knows what you need before you ask him.' There is such a sense of release in that. Yet it doesn't keep us from asking. In the Matthew context, the verse is not a deterrent but a stimulus to prayer. As Alexander Maclaren said, 'The devout soul does not argue "Thou knowest, and I need not speak," but "Thou knowest, therefore I tell thee."'[3] Or, simply: God knows, I tell.

This compulsion drives the child of God. In 1894, Elisha Hoffman was pastoring a Presbyterian church in Vassar, Michigan. He visited an elderly lady who was facing severe difficulties. She shared her problems with Hoffman, who in turn tried to comfort her, pointing her to particular biblical texts. He urged her to pray and tell her problems to Jesus. Somehow that suggestion seemed to stick—she smiled and said, 'Yes, I must tell Jesus.'

As Hoffman was on his way home her words kept repeating themselves, 'I must tell Jesus.' Other lines fell into place along with a singable tune.[4] And so we have …

> I must tell Jesus all of my trials;
> I cannot bear my burdens alone;
> In my distress he kindly will help me;
> He ever loves and cares for his own.
>
> I must tell Jesus! I must tell Jesus!
> I cannot bear my burdens alone;
> I must tell Jesus! I must tell Jesus!
> Jesus can help me, Jesus alone.

---

3   Alexander Maclaren, *The Psalms*, 3 vols. (reprint ed., Minneapolis: Klock & Klock, 1981), 1:381.
4   William J. Reynolds, *Songs of Glory* (Grand Rapids: Zondervan, 1990), p. 123.

Next, in verses 15-22, we find **a patient confidence for an urgent need**. One can translate the first particle in verse 15 various ways: 'But,' 'Indeed,' or 'Because.' I've chosen the last. His 'because' explains why he has been so 'deaf' and 'dumb' (vv. 13-14), why he has taken no initiative to break free from his twisted circumstances, namely, *because* he is waiting for Yahweh to intervene.[5]

Notice the 'wrapping' around this section: in verse 15, David uses three terms for God, 'Yahweh,' 'Lord' (Adonai), and 'my God.' Then he uses the same three terms at the close in verses 21-22. At the first he says, 'I have *waited*' (v. 15), but at the end he pleads, 'Hurry' (v. 22). In between he includes four—what we might call—semi-arguments that indicate why he is confident that Yahweh will 'answer' him (v. 15b).

David begins in verse 16 by suggesting that Yahweh must answer him for otherwise *my enemies would rejoice*. In verse 17, he implies Yahweh must intervene because *my collapse is near*. Verse 18 is not so much an argument as a consideration: *my guilt is confessed*, that is, there is no wrong that I am hiding or covering up. Then there is the matter of the sheer injustice of his affliction: *my attackers are in the wrong* (vv. 19-20). All this is a normal pattern for Psalm-praying: marshalling reasons for God to put things right.

But perhaps the most cogent reason for confidence may seem an indirect one. Remember the three ways David addressed the Lord in verses 15 and 21-22. One of those terms was 'my God' (vv. 15, 21). We might ponder

---

5   See Alec Motyer, *Psalms by the Day* (Ross-shire: Christian Focus, 2016), p. 101.

the importance of that. Let's come at the matter from the back door.

Major Thomas Jackson (later General 'Stonewall' Jackson) in about 1853 realized that he had fallen in love with Eleanor (Ellie) Junkin, a real 'catch,' since she was both deeply religious and terribly fun-loving. Ellie had an older sister, Margaret (Maggie), and they were inseparable friends as well. They dressed alike, shared the same room, took walks together, rode horses together, shared their most intimate secrets. Maggie was not charmed over Jackson's matrimonial intentions toward her sister. It really became a bit of a crisis but sufficient peace ensued so that Jackson and Ellie were married. But Maggie went along with them on their honeymoon![6] Before you condemn Maggie, realize that she may have had her defense: Why, she's *my sister* and we're closer than two crows on a piece of roadkill!

Now when David calls Yahweh 'my God,' does it not imply the same sort of inseparable relation? If Yahweh is his God, will He not be to him and for him all that God ought to be—even in the most contorted and grotesque of circumstances? Isn't there something of a solid assurance simply in David being able to say 'my God' here? I recall once reading Alexander Maclaren's exposition of 1 Samuel 30. That's the passage at the end of David's scrapes and escapes, the sour capstone of all his multiplied and ongoing troubles from 1 Samuel 18 on. David and his men have just enjoyed the relief of not having to fight against their own people (1 Sam. 29), and, after a sixty-mile trek back to Ziklag, they find the town

---

6   S. C. Gwynne, *Rebel Yell* (New York: Scribner, 2014), pp. 142-45.

burned and wives and children taken captive. It seemed like the ultimate punch in the gut. David himself becomes the object of the blame game. Then the narrator writes: 'Then David strengthened himself in Yahweh his God' (1 Sam. 30:6). Maclaren picked up on that text and wrote that David could no longer say 'my house,' 'my city,' or 'my possessions,' but he could still say 'my God.' Isn't that always the believer's firmest assurance?

Psalm 39

For the music leader. For Jeduthun. A psalm. David's.

(1) I said, 'I will keep guard on my ways
    —from sinning with my tongue;
  I will keep guard—a muzzle for my mouth,
    while the wicked is in front of me.'

(2) I remained dumb—silence;
  I was silent—without success,
  and my pain was stirred up.

(3) My heart was hot within me,
  while I was musing the fire would burn.
  I spoke with my tongue!

(4) Make me know, Yahweh, my end,
  (make me know) the measure of my days
    —what it is;
  let me know how fleeting I am!

(5) Look, you have made my days mere handbreadths,
  and my life-span as nothing before you.
  Surely every man, (even if) standing firm,
    is nothing but breath. Selah.

(6) Surely every man walks around as a shadow.
  Surely they make such a stir for nothing
    —he heaps up (stuff) and never knows who will gather (it).

(7) And now—what do I hope for, Lord?
  My hope—it is fixed on you.

(8) Deliver me from all my rebellions;
do not set me up so fools can ridicule me.

(9) I remained dumb—I did not open my mouth,
For **you** had done (it).

(10) Take away your plague from me;
because of the hostility of your hand
I have been finished off.

(11) With rebukes for iniquity you discipline a man
and you consume like a moth what he finds desirable.
Surely every man is nothing but breath! Selah.

(12) Hear my prayer, Yahweh,
and lend your ear to my cry for help;
don't be silent toward my tears;
for I am a sojourner with you,
a settler like all my fathers.

(13) Look away from me and let me cheer up,
before I go off and am no more.

A Little *Hevel* Is Healthy

2

Hevel. The word occurs three times in Psalm 39 (vv. 5, 6, 11). It refers primarily to what is transitory, fleeting, temporary, passing, non-lasting. Something like that may spawn reactions of futility or a sense of emptiness. But the primary meaning points to basic transitoriness and relative brevity.[1]

Most of us are familiar with *hevel.* We ourselves are currently in the middle of another house move. My wife has five sets of china inherited from sundry ancestors near and more remote. Will she move them to the next home? Oh yes, but she knows they're *hevel.* None of our children are going to want sets of china. Entertaining is much more informal now. There may be sentiment involved, because

---

1   See the discussion in Daniel C. Fredericks, *Coping with Transience: Ecclesiastes on Brevity in Life* (Sheffield: JSOT Press, 1993), pp. 11-32. You will sometimes find the word transliterated *hebel*, but the 'b' is soft and so is pronounced *hevel* (short e's).

these were one's grandmother's settings, but, truth be told, after our tenure runs out, the kids will hustle them off to the recycle bin. China is *hevel*. And why hang on to tools or equipment that haven't been used in five years? Its time is up. I have shelves of notebooks containing gobs of my biblical study and teaching/preaching notes, but, though useful to me, they will be of no help to others and will fill up the paper bin at the local dump. Stuff doesn't last; it's transitory. But it's not just stuff—seems people can be *hevel*: 'Surely every man... is nothing but breath [*hevel*]' (v. 5). That may give us problems, which is why we should walk with David through Psalm 39.

First, notice how he depicts **his impossible position** (vv. 1-3). He had determined, he says, that he would guard his speech, he would muzzle himself 'while the wicked is in front of me' (v. 1d). Apparently he feared that if he spoke openly of his distress and trouble, he might say something wrong, something rash, something that the wicked could pick up on and use to mock or disparage Yahweh. We meet something like this in Psalm 73. The psalmist there goes on from verses 4 to 14 complaining of the prosperity of the wicked and the uselessness of his own piety—then he says in verse 15: Now if I had talked openly like what I've just written, I would have brought harm to the Lord's own people; I could have terribly discouraged them. That is, there are times when our most faithful response is to keep our mouths shut. The same sort of restraint, in principle, seems to be operating here.

So, silence (v. 2a). 'I was silent,' he says in verse 2b, literally, 'from good.' The phrase is perplexing but I think Kidner has caught the gist of it in 'without success' (reflected in my translation). That is, I was silent but I couldn't hold it in; my pain and inner turmoil (vv. 2c-3) was simply too much—so 'I spoke with my tongue.' His intention was commendable but impossible to execute. The whole trouble he felt had to explode and come out.

Here we must 'cheat' and run over into verse 4: 'Make me know, Yahweh, my end,' etc. He 'spoke with (his) tongue' (v. 3c). And what did he speak? Prayer! Verse 4 begins his address to Yahweh and runs through verse 13. But it's important to simply let verse 4a hit you in the face. Whether the 'wicked' were around or not, he turns away from his vow of silence and pours out his trouble to Yahweh (vv. 4ff). This is so elementary and so important and yet can be made trivial and trite in the wrong hands. Sometimes the 'Well, just pray about it' advice we get from friends trivializes rather than honors prayer. It's almost equivalent to 'Have you taken your antacids today?' But here, after the agony of verses 1-3, prayer (4a) is the release needed. Prayer is the way ahead out of his impossible dilemma.

This psalm situation reminds me of a trip Barbara and I took during my third year of seminary. We were living in Iowa; I was to preach on a Sunday morning at a church in Steamboat Rock, a small town maybe 150 miles away. It was winter. It was snowing heavily.

Roads were snow covered. We had to allow plenty of time and drive carefully. The initial ordeal appeared to be over as we at last neared the town. We entered a left curve in the road and, though only going twenty-five miles an hour, I felt the rear tires going into a skid, wanting to place us somewhere over the right shoulder of the road. Then we noticed, off to the right of the curve, a small side street of the town, snow-covered but visible.

A slight steering adjustment took us out of the curve and skid and plunged us nicely into the relief of that street. It was the 'way through' our difficulty. That is the solution verse 4a gives here to the pent-up angst of verses 1-3. Not in the flippant sense of 'just pray about it.' But, as if to say in a glad and reverent tone, 'You can take this to the Lord in prayer.' We easily forget that prayer is the first step in walking through—and perhaps out of—our troubles.

In the following section we see **his increasing insight** (vv. 4-6). He begins with petition:

> Make me know, Yahweh, my end,
> (make me know) the measure of my days
> —what it is;
> let me know how fleeting I am! (v. 4).

He means 'make me know' in the sense 'Let me be impressed with,' so that it all comes home to me. He knows he cannot know the actual number of days left to him, but he can be rightly 'grabbed' by how relatively brief they are. He moves from petition to affirmation in verse 5a:

> Look, you have made my days mere handbreadths,
> and my life-span as nothing before you.

So it has 'come home' to him.

We might ask why. We may have a clue in verses 10-11, if we may read ahead a bit. He speaks of Yahweh's 'plague' upon him, of the 'hostility of [his] hand,' of 'rebukes for iniquity.' It may well be he was suffering physical affliction or illness that God imposed as chastisement for sin. If so, we can understand his fixation on how transitory his life is in verses 4-5. It sometimes only takes a good case of the flu to make a normally healthy fellow suddenly turn philosophical. How much more those afflicted with ongoing physical limitations, even if they are not necessarily connected with direct divine discipline. In any case, it seems Yahweh has stricken down our psalmist and this brings on a graphic sense of how terminally fragile he is.

But then he exclaims, 'But I'm not the only one—this is the way it is across the board!' Everyone, he says, is in this fix and one wonders if they are really aware of it. It all comes out in three statements in verses 5b-6, each of which begins with the same Hebrew particle (*'ak*), which I've translated 'surely':

> Surely every man, (even if) standing firm,
>   is nothing but breath [*hevel*].
> Surely every man walks around as a shadow.
> Surely they make such a stir for nothing [*hevel*]
>   —he heaps up (stuff) and never knows who will
>   gather (it).

NJPS translates the last statement,

> mere futility is his hustle and bustle,
> amassing and not knowing who will gather in.

What a word picture! It may bring to mind frantic shoppers pressing through the mall at Christmas time—but it's far broader than that. God's discipline has impressed on him the brevity of his life (vv. 4-5a) but also the fleeting futility of the life of all men, obviously taking in the wicked (vv. 5b-6). And he seems astonished, as if to say, 'I don't think they're aware of it.'

Jesus left us a 'cartoon' of such a fellow (Luke 12:16-20). He thought because of his prosperity that he was 'set' for 'many years' (v. 19), unaware that God was pulling the plug 'this night' (v. 20). I always think of the blind arrogance of presidential nominee John F. Kennedy. He did not want Lyndon Johnson on the ticket as Vice President but felt it could not be avoided. So he minimized the distaste when he told a colleague, 'I'm forty-three years old. I'm not going to die in office. So the vice presidency doesn't mean anything.'[2] Little did he know. Contrast that with the story I told in my commentary on Luke, of a younger friend and mother, suffering the ravages of cancer, who wrote and sang a song (accompanied on her guitar) called 'Just One More Christmas, Jesus.' Completely aware that her days were mere handbreadths, she sang her prayer that her Savior would yet give her one more Christmas with her children.[3] If our life is a 'mist' (James 4:14), we do well to act like it is.

Now we can consider **his true hope** (vv. 7-13). Verse 7 is the turning-point of the psalm; here, he anchors himself on the Lord. And it seems we can trace something of his thinking from this point.

He begins with his primary petition: 'Deliver me from all my rebellions; do not set me up so fools can ridicule me' (v. 8). Guilt matters more than circumstances; hence he wants to be free from 'rebellions,' from guilt and wrong. This, however, in no way eclipses his secondary petition (vv. 9-11), which focuses on the physical ravages Yahweh must have inflicted: 'your plague,' the 'hostility of your hand', and the way Yahweh 'disciplines.' David

---

2   Seymour M. Hersh, *The Dark Side of Camelot* (Boston: Little, Brown & Co., 1997), p. 130.
3   Dale Ralph Davis, *Luke 1–13: The Year of the Lord's Favor* (Ross-shire: Christian Focus, 2021), p. 224.

begs for freedom from 'your plague'—from the illness or disease or bodily chastisement Yahweh imposed.

He renews his plea to be heard and goes on to append a couple of collateral arguments. When he says, 'Hear my prayer' (v. 12a), I think he refers primarily to the petitions of verses 4, 8, and 10, and he implies that the Lord should consider his tears (v. 12b) and his status (v. 12c) in consenting to his request. When he says, 'Don't be silent toward my tears,' he seeks to arouse Yahweh's pity toward his suffering, hoping He will be moved to relieve it. Think of the graphic way he prays in Psalm 56:8: 'You keep count of my wanderings; put my tears in your bottle; are they not in your book?' David's God is a God who can count; tears and tragedies and troubles are not forgotten; it's as if Yahweh has a bottle to collect them, a book for recording them. Our tears are claims on the compassions of God.

But David pleads his status as well: 'for I am a sojourner with you, a settler like all my fathers' (v. 12b). That fits with the tone of the psalm—a sojourner, a settler; that's part of the brevity-of-life theme. There's more here, however. I think David turns this into an argument for answering prayer. You remember perhaps how Abraham used this lingo with the folks around Hebron? After Sarah died, he told them, 'I am a sojourner and settler among you' (Gen. 23:4). These are the words used here in verse 12: a sojourner (*ger*) is one who did not enjoy the rights of a resident; he was an alien; a 'settler' (*toshav*) is one who has no land of his own but is settled upon that of another, essentially a tenant. Life can be a hit-and-miss affair for sojourners and settlers. Yet one can't read David's words here without recalling what Yahweh told Israel in Leviticus 25:23: 'The land must not be sold beyond reclaim, for the land is mine—for you are sojourners and settlers [same words as in verse 12] with me.' Israelites were to consider themselves sojourners and settlers under Yahweh their landlord. But did you notice the 'with me'? Sojourners and settlers 'with me'? What does that imply? The 'sojourner' element may imply that one still has a fragile and temporary existence but it is 'with me', i.e., with Yahweh, indicating that I am a sojourner/settler under His special care and protection.[4] How could it be otherwise? For Yahweh had commanded Israel to show special compassion to sojourners (Deut. 10:18-19), so surely Yahweh Himself must follow His own law! That is the 'argument' David presses on Yahweh: True, I am as fragile and precarious as a mere sojourner, but there's a difference—I am a sojourner and settler *with you*! You then, he implies, have an obligation and commitment to me. You might do well to carry around those last two lines of verse 12 in your hip pocket—you may want to use them as a part of your own appeals.

Let's catch up. Verse 7 is the turning-point in our psalm. After that David urges his primary petition (v. 8), his secondary petition (vv. 9-11), then his collateral arguments (v. 12)—and now ends with verse 13: 'Look away from me and let me cheer up, before I go off and am no more.'[5] Does that sound like a disappointment? Something of a let-down after walking through this whole psalm?

---

4   John E. Hartley, *Leviticus*, Word Biblical Commentary (Dallas: Word, 1992), p. 437.
5   NET renders it: 'Turn your angry gaze away from me, so I can be happy before I pass away.'

In the nineteenth century, the United States and Canada had various boundary disputes. On one occasion, the Americans spent three years building a fort at the northern end of Lake Champlain only to find out in 1818 that it stood on the Canadian side of the boundary and had to be evacuated.[6] Such a let-down after all the effort and work. And verse 13 may seem a let-down to the psalm reader. Is this what David settles for? To have some 'space' from his pressures, to be relieved from his crushing load, so he can have a bit of cheer and happiness, an interim of relief in the present days? After all he prays for, is he content with only this?

But what's wrong with 'only this'? What's wrong with wanting a tenure of relief without the plague of illness or sickness? What's wrong with being able to smile a little even though the brevity of life hangs over us? Why can't we sometimes be free from the wicked breathing down our necks? What's wrong with an interval of cheerfulness in the *hevel* of life? Alec Motyer has said it well: 'The brevity of life and the sadness of death run throughout the Bible and the full revelation of the immortal world does not remove them. This life is precious. Its joys and loves may be transcended but they cannot be replaced.'[7] Therefore we should plead to enjoy these joys and loves.

6   Daniel Walker Howe, *What Hath God Wrought* (Oxford: University Press, 2007), p. 96.
7   J. A. Motyer, 'The Psalms,' in *New Bible Commentary*, 4th ed. (Leicester: Inter-Varsity, 1994), p. 511.

Psalm 40

For the music leader. David's. A psalm.

(1) I simply waited for Yahweh,
  and he turned to me
    and heard my cry for help.

(2) And he brought me up from the raging pit,
      out of the muck and mire,
    and set my feet upon a rock
      —he made my steps secure,

(3) and he put a new song in my mouth
      of praise to our God;
    many will see and fear
      and trust in Yahweh.

(4) How blessed the man who makes Yahweh his trust,
    who does not turn to the arrogant
      and those turning after a lie.

(5) You have done **many things**, Yahweh, my God,
      your wonders and your thoughts toward us
    —there is no way of rehearsing them to you;
    I want to tell and speak
      —they are too many to mention!

(6) Sacrifice and offering you have not wanted
      —**ears** you have dug for me;
    burnt-offering and sin-offering you have not asked for.

(7) Then I said,
      'Look, I come,
      in the scroll of the book it is written for me;

(8) I delight to do your will, O my God,
   and your teaching is deep within me.'

(9) I have declared the glad news of righteousness
      in the great congregation;
   indeed, I will not hold back my lips,
      O Yahweh, **you** know.

(10) I have not covered up your righteousness
       within my heart;
    your faithfulness and your salvation I have told;
    I have not concealed your unfailing love and your faithfulness
       from the great congregation.

(11) **You**, Yahweh, you will not hold back
       your compassions from me;
    your unfailing love and your faithfulness
       will continually preserve me.

(12) For evils—beyond number—have surrounded me,
    my iniquities have overtaken me
       and I cannot see;
    they are more than the hairs of my head,
       and my heart fails me.

(13) Be pleased, Yahweh, to deliver me;
    Yahweh, hurry to help me.

(14) Let them be ashamed and abashed together
       who seek my life, to sweep it away;
    let them be turned back and humiliated
       who get pleasure in my distress.

(15) Let them be horrified due to their shame
       who say to me, 'Aha! Aha!'

(16) Let all who seek you rejoice and be glad in you;
    Let those who love your salvation continually say,
       'How great Yahweh is!'

(17) But I am poor and needy;
    the Lord will take thought for me.
    You are my help and my escape;
    O my God, do not delay.

3

A Lot of Waiting

Put up with some lore from American baseball. In 1952, Virgil Trucks was a pitcher for the Detroit Tigers. He racked up some remarkable achievements that year. In May, he pitched a no-hitter against the Washington Senators, and in August, he no-hit the formidable New York Yankees. In another game against Washington, he gave up a hit to the first batter and then pitched a no-hitter the rest of the game. And yet Trucks' record for the year was a dismal five wins and nineteen losses. A combination of brilliant achievements and disappointing failures. Psalm 40 is a bit like that. David rehearses a dazzling deliverance Yahweh worked in the first half of the psalm, and yet, near the end, it looks like the mud and mire are beginning to gather under his feet again. There was marvelous relief followed by more dire need. A bit of a 'mixed bag.' Our task, of course, is to listen to what David is telling us in the psalm.

First, he passes on **a bracing testimony** (vv. 1-5). He begins by telling us, literally, 'Waiting, I waited on Yahweh.' It's a grammatical construction meant to stress the 'waiting.' English translations tend to translate 'waited patiently,' but I agree with Alec Motyer: he is just saying that waiting is what he did. 'I simply waited for Yahweh.' 'And he turned to me'—what glorious attention! The usual 'he inclined to me' is a bit stodgy. Rather, He 'turned to me'; one could almost translate, 'He bent down to me.' Then David offers that graphic picture of Yahweh's deliverance:

And he brought me up from the raging pit,
    out of the muck and mire,
and set my feet upon a rock
    —he made my steps secure,
and he put a new song in my mouth
    of praise to our God (vv. 2-3a).

He took me, David says, from slime to security to song. If you put credence in David's authorship of the psalm (and I see no reason not to do so), you can find ample muck-and-mire-and-deliverance episodes in 1 Samuel 18-30. Even the praise for deliverance (a new song) is a gift from Yahweh. And it all has a ripple effect: 'many will see and fear and trust in Yahweh' (v. 3b). Yahweh's 'pit-removal' for me will encourage others to lean on Him, David says. Of course, David says, my experience is only one of *many* that Yahweh does for His people (v. 5a); in fact, He leaves us with the happy frustration of having too many instances to mention (v. 5b)! As Joseph Addison's hymn says, 'For oh, eternity's too short to utter all your praise.'[1]

---

1   From 'When All Your Mercies, O My God,' *Trinity Psalter Hymnal* (2018), No. 237.

This testimony is not one of those back-there-in-Bible-times affairs. Yahweh repeatedly gives His people, post-David, occasions to repeat verses 2-3a as their own testimony. The particulars may vary, but the testimony is essentially the same. Sometimes there's a human agent. John Staupitz was such for Martin Luther. Sometimes Luther could take six hours confessing his sins, and Staupitz would almost rail at Luther, telling him God was not angry with him but that he was angry with God and that he could not see God's free and undeserved mercy extended to him in Christ. Luther said of Staupitz, 'He gave birth to me in Christ. If Staupitz had not helped me, I would have been swallowed up in hell and left there.'[2] But God brought him up out of the muck and mire.

Sometimes, of course, the muck and mire have an extended tenure. It was 1841 when J. C. Ryle's father lost everything in bad bank dealings. J. C. Ryle himself was twenty-five and says,

> [I] lost everything, and saw the whole future of my life turned upside down, and thrown into confusion. In short if I had not been a Christian at this time, I do not know if I should not have committed suicide.[3]

Literally overnight, Ryle was slammed into the mire— friends of his father offered Ryle and a sister a place to stay. He soon went toward the ministry, not because he craved it but because it seemed the only living available to him. But he saw that was the way God brought him out of his

---

2   N. R. Needham, *2000 Years of Christ's Power,* 5 vols. (Ross-shire: Christian Focus Publications, 2004), 3:72.

3   Iain H. Murray, *J. C. Ryle: Prepared to Stand Alone* (Edinburgh: Banner of Truth, 2016), p. 49.

pit—he confessed that if he had not been ruined, he would never have preached a sermon, or written a tract or book. God had a 'rock' for him. One has the sense, however, that Ryle always winced when he remembered being 'ruined.'

But this is not only for Luthers and Ryles. I can myself testify with David. Oh, I can't say I had cried for help (v. 1), for I hadn't. I can't say I was 'waiting' on Yahweh. But in His kind providence He dipped His hands into the muck and mire I was beginning to enjoy. You don't need the particular details. It's a testimony hordes of the saints can repeat.

Secondly, David tells us what **a glad commitment** he makes to Yahweh (vv. 6-10). This is only proper; after the star-spangled deliverance of verses 2-3 and the countless additional mercies of verse 5, the text almost shouts at us: In view of all this, what sort of response does God want?

To answer that, we have to think about the difference *ears* make (v. 6a). He says, 'Sacrifice and offering you have not wanted—ears you have dug for me.' English translations make it sound a bit better, but 'ears you have dug' is a literal rendering. An ear is a responsive body part, reacting to or receiving what is heard. Probably the most fruitful cross-reference is in the third 'Servant Song' in Isaiah 50:4, where the Servant begins speaking about a tongue but soon ends up with an ear:

> The Lord Yahweh has given to me a tongue of disciples
>   to know (how) to sustain the weary with a word;
> he wakens, morning by morning,
>   he wakens my ear to hear as disciples do.

He seems to mean that in order to speak as one of Yahweh's disciples and to speak in such a way as to sustain the weary and downcast, he must first have an ear that submissively receives the Word Yahweh communicates to him. That note of submission seems to be in our psalm. 'Ears you have dug for me' says that Yahweh has given him the right response, a submissive response to Yahweh's Word.

However, to understand David's response we also need to know the difference a *scroll* makes. That may sound wild, but I didn't write the psalm! So in verses 7-8 we hear …

> Then I said,
>> 'Look, I come,
>> in the scroll of the book it is written for me;
>> I delight to do your will, O my God,
>> and your teaching [torah] is deep within me.'

Here's what I think is the simplest explanation of 'the scroll of the book.' Remember that David (again, accrediting his authorship here) is the covenant king. And in Yahweh's covenant law there was a regulation for Israel's king(s). It's in Deuteronomy 17:14-20. When David says (v. 7) that it is 'written for me,' he doesn't mean 'written about me,' but 'written *for* me,' that is, 'prescribed for me to do.' When David speaks of the scroll of the book he refers to this royal job description Yahweh lays down for kings in Deuteronomy 17, which says there are two marks that should characterize any future Israelite king. He should be *different* (Deut. 17:16-17)—he does not salivate over weapons, women, or wealth.[4] The usual perks of near eastern kingship (military muscle, massive harems, royal riches) do not drive him. And he should be *submissive*,

---

4   Chris Wright, *Deuteronomy*, New International Biblical Commentary (Peabody, MA: Hendrickson, 1996), p. 209.

submissive to Yahweh's covenant law. Which is why the king is to write out his own copy of the covenant law and read it regularly, so that it will govern his own attitude and conduct (Deut. 17:18-20). That's what, I think, David refers to here. Indeed, David claims Yahweh's law is not merely his reading material, but it has captured him— 'I delight to do your will ... your torah is deep within me.'

If this view holds water, then David is saying that he seeks to embody Yahweh's design for his king. And the following context shows *how* he does Yahweh's will (v. 8) at this point—by declaring among God's worshiping people (vv. 9-10) the kindness and faithfulness of God in His deliverance (remember vv. 1-3).

What we have in the commitment of Psalm 40:6-8 is simply an Old Testament version of Romans 12:1. Perhaps you've read how J. B. Phillips translated the first of that verse: 'With eyes wide open to the mercies of God ...' The 'mercies of God' are what Paul had just itemized in the previous eleven chapters of Romans, telling us of an impossible God who 'justifies the ungodly' (4:5), who has determined to shape us into the likeness of Jesus (8:29), and who refuses to abandon His original covenant people on the ash heap of history (ch. 11)—now, in view of this God and these mercies, what should your response be? 'Present your bodies a sacrifice—living, holy, pleasing to God, your logical worship.' That's David's response here in the psalm. Surely you can catch the joy and delight that pulsates in verses 6-8—it is the logical response for the mercies of verses 1-3 and 5.

Carl Sandburg tells of the White House reception held on the evening of President Lincoln's second inauguration. It was March 1865. The War between the States was nearing its end. Lincoln spent some three hours in handshaking. Packed into this unending line to greet the President were Adelaide Smith and a certain Lieutenant Gosper. They were apparently an 'item.' Gosper's right leg had been shot off in a skirmish at Petersburg, Miss Smith was the nurse who had looked after him, and a very close relationship had blossomed. Finally, they got near the President, Lt. Gosper hobbling on his crutch. Much to their surprise in this pedantic procedure, Lincoln stepped out in front of them, took the hand of Lt. Gosper and in a voice said to be unforgettable exclaimed, 'God bless you, my boy!' Gosper was deeply moved. As the couple moved on he told Miss Smith, 'Oh! I'd lose another leg for a man like that!'[5] That seems like David's attitude here, as if he would say, Oh, I delight to do the will of a God like that! A God like verses 1-3 speak of. Isn't that really the explanation of our own glad commitment? Isn't it true that, like the apostle Paul, we can just never cease talking to ourselves about 'the Son of God who loved me and gave himself for me' (Gal. 2:20)?

Third, David speaks of **a fresh urgency** he faces (vv. 11-17). Verse 11 is an indicative statement, a piece of assurance, and not a request or petition as in the NIV or NKJV. Here, he plays off a verb he used in verse 9. There, he had said, 'I will not hold back my lips' from testifying of God's goodness. Now, in verse 11, he affirms, 'You [emphatic], Yahweh, will not hold back your compassions from me.' Why does he need such compassions?

---

5   Carl Sandburg, *Abraham Lincoln: The Prairie Years and the War Years.* One volume ed. (New York: Harcourt, Brace & Jovanovich, 1974), p. 665.

Apparently, because circumstances have changed, as verse 12 explains: 'For evils—beyond number—have surrounded me.'

What 'evils'? First, there are the evils within (v. 12):

[M]y iniquities have overtaken me
    and I cannot see;
they are more than the hairs of my head
    and my heart fails me.

We are accustomed in the Psalms to hearing of the evil coming from external attack—and David faces more of that here (vv. 14-15); but he does not ignore the distress that his own guilt has brought upon him, though he does not satisfy our curiosity with any lurid details. So there are evils within (v. 12) and evils without (vv. 14-15). In this whole section, then, we find that he prays for himself (v. 13), he prays against his enemies (vv. 14-15), he prays for the saints (v. 16), and he prays for himself again (v. 17). And time is of the essence (v. 17b).

Some readers (and some critics) may wonder how all the buoyancy of verses 1-10 could so soon evaporate and a bit of thanksgiving for deliverance could suddenly turn into a plea for more of the same. But this is simply biblical realism. To be lifted out of the muck doesn't mean there won't be more muck.[6]

One of the favorite games of President Theodore Roosevelt and his sons was the 'point-to-point hike.' This

---

6 Alexander Maclaren (*The Psalms*, 3 vols. [reprint ed., Minneapolis: Klock & Klock, 1981], 2:27) rightly asks: 'Are there any deliverances in this perilous and incomplete life so entire and permanent that they leave no room for future perils? Must not prevision of coming dangers accompany thankfulness for past escapes?'

meant they picked an objective to reach, then went in a straight line toward it, which meant going over, under, or through whatever stood in the path. Sometimes it could be formidable. Once, Roosevelt invited French ambassador Jean-Jules Jusserand to go on a walk and explained it was a point-to-pointer. All was well till they came to the bank of a stream, too wide and deep to be easily crossed. Jusserand thought this would be the conclusion but, horrified, realized 'TR' was taking off his clothes. He told Jusserand that they'd better strip so as not to get their things wet in the creek. Jusserand said then that he too, 'for the honor of France,' removed his clothes. Then they jumped in and swam across.[7]

That, however, is the way of believing experience. It's a sort of point-to-pointer. We should not then be surprised to find that sometimes doxologies must morph into supplications. Even so; for if Yahweh has delivered before, surely He is up for an encore.

Finally, David's psalm, in view of its 'after-life' in Hebrews 10, leads us to think of **a single sacrifice**. The writer of Hebrews was explaining how the sacrifices offered under the old covenant could never decisively deal with sin and guilt. Such repeated sacrifices *remind* of sin rather than *remove* sin (cf. 10:1-4). Then he quotes Psalm 40:6-7 as though they were the words of Christ Himself.[8]

---

7 Paul F. Boller, Jr., *Presidential Diversions* (Orlando: Harcourt, 2007), p. 180. Jusserand insisted on keeping his lavender kid gloves on, however, because, as he remarked, 'It would be embarrassing if we should meet ladies'!

8 The differences between LXX, which the writer of Hebrews quotes, and the Hebrew text do not affect the main point we are seeking to make.

The 'will' Christ does is to offer His body as the once-for-all sacrifice for sins (10:10).

Is then Psalm 40 a direct messianic psalm? I don't think so. How could Christ in any way confess that His iniquities had overtaken Him and were more than the hairs of His head (v. 12)? How are we to look at Jesus and the psalm then? We begin by remembering that if David has written the psalm, and if he is speaking as the covenant king in verses 6-8, then it would be perfectly appropriate for Jesus, David's royal descendant, who shared his office of covenant representative, to express the same uninhibited commitment to doing God's will—obviously at greater cost. Because Jesus shares the same 'office' as David, He can legitimately be said to share his whole-hearted commitment. Our psalm, I suppose we could say, is not completely messianic but covenantally messianic.

Now see where Hebrews takes all this. The writer refers to the priests in the Jerusalem temple, who stand every day, over and over offering the same sacrifices—with an element of futility, for they 'can never take away sins' (Heb. 10:11). Then comes the 'counter': 'But this [priest], when he had offered one sacrifice for sins for all time, sat down at the right hand of God' (Heb. 10:12). Note the posture: 'he sat down.' He sat down because His work was finished—there was no more to do. One decisive sacrifice—and guilt can no longer haunt His people.

Can you sense the relief in that—between ongoing futile measures and definite, decisive action? Many moons ago when I was a child, our family car was a rather old Chevrolet. It was, of course, a 'standard shift,' with the gear shift on the steering column. But my father found that in the process of shifting gears he was constantly breaking off the white, plastic gear shift handles normally used. Maybe in the cold Pennsylvania winters the temperature was too cold and those plastic handles proved too brittle. But then my dad found the solution. He cut off the end of a wooden shovel handle, about five or six inches of it, bored a hole part way in it, and pounded it on to the end of the gear shift! It had no aesthetic charm; it was what we sometimes call a 'red neck' affair. But it brought a total end to the irritatingly broken plastic gear shift handles. So when Jesus delighted to do God's will, He 'sat down,' because something decisive had occurred—nothing more ever needed to be done for your guilt.

Psalm 41

To the music leader. A psalm. David's.

(1) How blessed the one who pays attention to the helpless;
on a day of distress Yahweh will grant him escape.

(2) **Yahweh** will guard him and preserve him alive;
he will be blessed in the land.
And do not give him up to the desire of his enemies!

(3) **Yahweh** will sustain him on his sick-bed;
you have transformed all his bed in his illness.

(4) As for me, I said, 'Yahweh, show grace to me;
heal my soul, for I have sinned against you.'

(5) **My enemies** speak evil against me;
'When will he die and his name perish?'

(6) And when one comes to see (me) he speaks falsehood;
his heart gathers up wickedness for himself;
he goes outside (and) talks.

(7) All who hate me whisper together against me;
against me they scheme disaster for me.

(8) 'A horrid thing is being poured out on him,
and he will not rise up again from where he lies.'

(9) Even a man with whom I was at peace,
a man in whom I trusted,
one eating my bread,
has lifted (his) heel against me.

(10)   But **you**, Yahweh, show grace to me
      and raise me up,
    so that I might pay them back.

(11)   By this I know that you have delighted in me,
    that my enemy will not shout in triumph over me.

(12)   But as for me,
    in my whole-heartedness you have held on to me
    and have made me stand before you forever.

(13)   Blessed be Yahweh, God of Israel,
      from everlasting to everlasting.
     Amen and amen.

4

Of Blessing, Beds, and Betrayal

We've seen it before—this strange combination of
assurance and desperation. Here it is again in Psalm
41. It really shouldn't perplex us that much; real life
is full of unusual combinations. In the USA during
the Second World War, black leaders saw that the war
economy had put more African Americans to work than
ever before. One female black American put it crassly:
'Hitler was the one that got us out of the white folks'
kitchen.'[1] One usually doesn't think of Hitler as any sort
of benefactor for anyone. But there it is: the scourge of
Hitler strangely enough worked to the benefit of some
black Americans. Strange combinations are really quite
legion, so we don't need to swallow hard when we see
them in the Psalms.

---

1   A. J. Baime, *The Accidental President: Harry S. Truman and the Four
Months that Changed the World* (Boston: Mariner Books, 2018), p. 159.

Let's wade into the text: in verses 1-3, David tells us of **the position he takes**, what he holds to be so. He begins with a beatitude, 'How blessed the one who pays attention to the helpless.' 'Helpless' translates the Hebrew adjective *dal* that can refer to the poor, powerless, weak—to those deprived of resources, to the folks who don't seem to count for much. It's used, for example, to describe the emaciated cows Pharaoh saw in his dream (Gen. 41:19).[2] This 'blessed' one 'pays attention to' or 'considers' the helpless. Derek Kidner finds this striking, since the verb implies 'giving careful thought' to the person's situation and not some sort of flippant, fleeting notice.[3]

David expects this 'blessed' one to receive blessings, such as:

On a day of distress Yahweh will grant him escape (v. 1b)

Yahweh will guard him and preserve him alive;
he will be blessed in the land (v. 2a)

Yahweh will sustain him on his sick-bed (v. 3a).[4]

The upshot of verses 1-3 is an early version of 'Blessed are the merciful, for they shall obtain mercy' (Matt. 5:7).

---

2   See NIDOTTE, 1:951-52, and TWOT, 1:190.

3   Derek Kidner, *Psalms 1–72*, TOTC (London: Inter-Varsity, 1973), p. 161.

4   David also 'sneaks in' a one-liner prayer in 2b ('And do not give him up to the desire of his enemies'). The translation of v. 3b varies, as a check of translations shows. I've translated the verb, 'turned over,' as 'transformed,' implying healing from his illness. Cf. Allen Ross, *A Commentary on the Psalms,* 3 vols. (Grand Rapids: Kregel, 2011), 1:881: 'He means that God transformed the whole place where he was suffering by healing him. To change the bed in his sickness means to alleviate the sickness so the place is transformed.'

Now why does David tell us all this? I think he is being autobiographical. He is suggesting that he is one who pays attention to the helpless, and therefore he expects the assurances (noted above) to prove true in his case. David is the covenant king and as king he has responsibilities toward the needy. Psalm 72, ascribed to Solomon, sketches out what the ideal king would do. And David's words here imply that these are the sort of things he has done:

> For he delivers the needy when he calls for help,
>> including the afflicted and the one who has no one
>>> to help him;
> he has pity on the helpless [*dal*] and needy,
>> and saves the lives of the needy (Ps. 72:12-13).

Hence, he expects Yahweh to grant him escape (v. 1), protection (v. 2), and healing (v. 3). So in verses 1-3 David spells out, as I have indicated, the position he takes.

This 'position' is a superb place to stand. But the psalm goes on to show that it is a stance that will be tested—it will meet sins and enemies and betrayers (vv. 4-10). Those matters will show how the 'creed' of verses 1-3 shakes out under troubling circumstances. I suppose one could say that the faith-position we take has to be 'walked out' in adverse circumstances. Creed usually walks into conflict.

During the last years of Dr. Alexander Whyte's life, he wrote to Miss Innes, a sister of one of Whyte's closest friends. It is 1918, the closing weeks of World War I, and he writes briefly to Miss Innes: 'Could I be with you as of old, I might have much to say of my inmost life: here I will only say that what I preached so long to you is now the one stay and strength of my life.'[5] He was affirming that the faith he had proclaimed had proven solid amid the turmoil and difficulties of his life. We may pray to enjoy the same.

We move into the middle of the psalm. Here David relates **the plea he makes** (vv. 4-10). In verse 4a he tells us that his prayer began with 'Yahweh, show grace to me,' and in verse 10 he closes the petition with the same words. Cries for grace, then, wrap his lament.

His description of his condition focuses on human infidelity. He does not neglect his own infidelity but confesses it first: 'Heal my soul, for I have sinned against you' (v. 4b). He does not divulge what his sins were in this case. We don't need to know. But he does not blithely assume that all unfaithfulness is external. No, there is his own *guilt*, and he does not ignore it. He dwells, however, on the threat that his enemies pose, especially their *malice* (v. 5)—they simply cannot wait for him to die. And that malice is riddled with *insincerity* (vv. 6-7). It seems that when one of them makes a 'sick call,' there is a show of concern, but afterwards, the visitor goes out and blabs the intelligence gathered with his fellow conspirators, who, as David says, 'scheme disaster for me' (v. 7b). Apparently some severe sickness or extreme affliction had taken David. Verse 8 consists of the enemies' words— their dire prognosis: 'A horrid thing is being poured out on him, and he will not rise up again from where he lies.' They assume he is 'terminal.' 'A horrid thing' renders what is, literally, 'a thing of belial,' i.e., what is

5   G. F. Barbour, *The Life of Alexander Whyte D. D.* (London: Hodder and Stoughton, 1923), p. 605.

terribly wicked or abhorrent.[6] They claim that God has inflicted a horrendous punishment on him, from which there can be no recovery. So there is *sickness*. But worst of all—*betrayal* (v. 9). One of his closest, most trusted and intimate friends has joined the conspirators.[7] One can scarcely slide any lower.

So what does one do at that point, in the face of such a barrage of trouble and sneakiness? What can one do, except to say, 'Yahweh, show grace to me' (vv. 4, 10)? Let's come back to this, but first we need to note why he craves that 'grace' according to verse 10. There he says, 'Show grace to me and raise me up, so that I might pay them back.' 'Oh my,' someone wails, 'just like the *Old* Testament—David wants revenge; so against the spirit of the New Testament.' But before we have psychological apoplexy, let's consider that those opposing David are opposing Yahweh's designated covenant king. Therefore, they are both David's and Yahweh's enemies. And think about David. He is not merely some joe-schmo private citizen but the covenant king. It's his *job* to deal with such rebels (Ps. 101:7-8)

---

6   Cf. NIDOTTE, 1:662, and J. A. Motyer, *Psalms by the Day* (Ross-shire: Christian Focus, 2016), p. 109.

7   This could be an allusion to Ahithophel (2 Sam. 15:12, 31; 16:20-23; 17:1-14, 23), the Judas Iscariot of the Old Testament. Jesus alludes to this verse in John 13:18, as a Scripture 'fulfilled' in Judas' betrayal. This does not mean that Psalm 41 is 'all about Jesus' or that it is a 'messianic' psalm in the full sense. The psalmist's reference to his sins in verse 4 show that the psalm does not 'fit' Jesus in any total way. But David was the covenant king and the kind of troubles he faced in that capacity are the same sort that his covenant Descendant faced in the days of His flesh. What the original covenant king suffered was a harbinger of what the final covenant king would suffer.

and he has received promises of divine protection (Pss. 20:6; 89:22-23). Verse 10 is not speaking of his inflicting a personal vendetta but of carrying out his duty as covenant king.

But, once again, what can David do in the face of this assault and conspiracy against him? He can pray, 'Yahweh, show grace to me.' Is that all? It's so elementary, it seems, so terribly basic.

Once, on a South African flight on Kulula Airlines, the routine pre-flight announcement came with a twist. The voice said: 'Welcome aboard Kulula 271 to Port Elizabeth. To operate your seat belt, insert the metal tab into the buckle, and pull tight. It works just like every other seat belt; and, if you don't know how to operate one, you probably shouldn't be out in public unsupervised.' In short, if you can't handle something as basic as a seat belt, you forfeit your right to independent living! Basic ability is a clue to additional competence.

In the same way, 'Show grace to me' may seem very basic but is by no means trite. It is, we might say, where prayer begins. This particular verb form (from the root *hnn*, to show grace, be gracious) occurs twenty-one times in the Psalms in the face of a plethora of emergencies and troubles.[8] But the psalmists pray this way because they have a holy suspicion that God will in fact act 'grace-shuss-ly.' Note Psalm 86:15, where David repeats the 'creed' from Exodus 34:6-7, 'But you, Lord, are a God compassionate and *gracious*' (same root as our verb) and

---

8 For the record, in case you want to check them out: 4:1; 6:2; 9:13; 25:16; 26:11; 27:7; 30:10; 31:9; 41:4, 10; 51:1; 56:1; 57:1 [twice]; 86:3, 16; 119:29, 58, 132; 123:3 [twice].

then in the next verse turns that doctrine into prayer, 'Turn to me and show grace to me.' He expects grace from a gracious God.[9]

It may seem too rudimentary, too simple, but what better plea can one bring in all our own guilt or in the face of the malice, hatred, and betrayal of others to a God who already has a grace-bent to His nature?

After his extended description and petition, David speaks of **the assurance he obtains** (vv. 11-12). One could call it two-fold assurance. We might say that verse 11 speaks of 'negative' assurance, that is, assurance David gets because of what did—or would—*not* happen. He knows Yahweh has delighted in him because his enemy has not won the day (v. 11).

Verse 12, however, might be dubbed 'positive' assurance:

But as for me,
in my whole-heartedness you have held on to me
and have made me stand before you forever.

The 'whole-heartedness' bothers some readers.[10] After all, didn't David confess sin in verse 4? But 'whole-heartedness' is not sinlessness nor perfection; he only claims that this is the overall bent of his life—that he has not turned away from his devotion to Yahweh. And what has he found? That Yahweh has 'held on to' His servant. How much more secure can one be? It brings to mind Jesus' blood-stirring assurance in John 10:27-28:

---

9   Or, as Psalm 119:132 puts it: 'Turn to me and show grace to me, *as is your custom* to those who love your name.'

10   The word is often translated 'integrity.' The root (*tmm*) refers to what is whole or 'all there.' Hence I translate it 'whole-heartedness.'

My sheep hear my voice,
and I know them,
and they follow me,
and I give them eternal life,
and they will never, ever perish,
and no one will rip them out of my hand.

And why is that? Because He holds on to them. 'You have held on to me'—that's what so gladdens David here. And, we have to say this is no mere episodic, incidental, present-case-only kind of security, for he goes on to say that you 'have made me stand before you forever.' Try to shrink-wrap or evaporate that with talk about how partial and limited Old Testament faith was; but, as a matter of fact, that sounds terribly solid and lasting.

Psalms 42-43

To the music leader. A maskil. Belonging to the sons of Korah.

42:1 As a deer longs for streams of water,
      so my soul longs for you, O God.

42:2 My soul thirsts for God,
          for the living God;
      when can I come
          and appear in the presence of God?

42:3 My tears have been my food
          day and night,
      while all day long they say to me,
          'Where is your God?'

42:4 Here's what I can remember
          as I pour out my soul:
      that I used to pass on in the throng,
      how I used to lead them to the house of God
          with the voice of shouting and praise,
          a multitude at festival.

42:5 Why are you cast down, my soul,
          and why so upset within me?
      Hope in God,
          for I will yet praise him
          for the salvation of his face.

42:6 O my God,
      My soul is cast down within me,
      therefore I remember you,
          from the land of Jordan and Hermon,
          from Mount Mizar.

42:7 Deep keeps calling to deep
    at the sound of your water-channels
  —all your breakers and your waves
    have rolled over me.

42:8 By day Yahweh commands his unfailing love
  and at night his song is with me,
    a prayer to the God of my life.

42:9 I say to God, my rock,
    'Why have you forgotten me?
  Why do I go round mourning
    because the enemy presses me down?

42:10 It's like crushing my bones
    when my foes mock me,
    when they say to me all day long,
      "Where is your God?"'

42:11 Why are you cast down, my soul,
  and why so upset within me?
  Hope in God,
    for I will yet praise him,
    the salvation of my face and my God.

43:1 Give me justice, O God,
  and plead my case against a nation without grace;
  rescue me from a deceitful and wicked man;

43:2 for you are my fortress-God
  —why have you rejected me?
  Why must I go round mourning
    because the enemy presses me down?

43:3 Send out your light and your truth
    —**they** can lead me;
  let them bring me to your holy hill
    and to your dwelling-place!

43:4 Then I will come to the altar of God,
    to God, my exceeding joy,
  and I will praise you with lyre,
    O God, my God.

43:5 Why are you cast down, my soul,
    and why so upset within me?
  Hope in God,
    for I will yet praise him,
    the salvation of my face and my God.

5

'FIGHTINGS AND FEARS WITHIN, WITHOUT'

Our chapter title comes from part of Charlotte Elliott's justly famous hymn, 'Just As I Am.' Some of us probably have a hard time appreciating this hymn, for we have memories of its being used as an 'invitation hymn' in various evangelistic meetings. If there was little or no response, no one 'coming forward,' the evangelist might up the pressure, telling us 'we're going to sing that first stanza one more time' [perhaps by now for the sixth time]. But it was not originally an 'evangelistic' hymn; rather it was an exercise in which Miss Elliott was seeking to set out the basis of her own assurance.[1] And she captured a good bit of the believer's life with

> though tossed about
> with many a conflict,
>   many a doubt,
> fightings and fears within, without ....

---

1   See Elsie Houghton, *Christian Hymn-writers* (Bridgend: Evangelical Press of Wales, 1982), pp. 208-212.

It's the believer's see-saw battle between despair and hope, and it pretty well sums up the movement of Psalms 42–43.

We can track our way through these psalms via a few key words. The first is **appetite**, clearly expressed in the first two verses:

> As a deer longs for streams of water,
> so my soul longs for you, O God.
> My soul thirsts for God,
>   for the living God;
> when can I come
>   and appear in the presence of God?

We can be oblivious, however, to the fact that such thirst involves *pain*. Sinclair Ferguson helps us to see this:

> But we sometimes forget that the kind of thirst for God of which the Bible speaks is also a terrible experience. It means that we feel a famine of his presence, and absence of his grace and power. Spiritual thirst is painful, not pleasant; it may produce melancholy, not melody in our lives.[2]

So, although thirst for God seems a positive matter, it also implies want, deficiency, and a certain sadness. But something else is surprising here. The psalm assumes this thirst will be satiated at a *place*. The language 'appear in the presence of God' (v. 2b) harks back to texts in Exodus (23:17; 34:23), where it refers to appearing at the sanctuary, at the place of public worship. This is counter-cultural for contemporary 'evangelical Christians.' We

---

2   Sinclair B. Ferguson, *Deserted by God?* (Grand Rapids: Baker, 1993), p. 53.

are so geared to associating God's presence with special occasions: perhaps private devotional times, when you take your favorite study Bible, devotional book, and cup of caffeine to a quiet place; or special events in the life of the church—singles' retreats or married couples' retreats or keenagers' (a euphemism for older people) retreats or Bible conferences or cruises hosted by fine evangelical organizations. But the text implies that the presence of God is at the central sanctuary. In our lingo, church. That may strike a negative note. After all, lots of churches have lots of stuff wrong with them and no church is so exemplary that one cannot find something wrong with it. We tend to think that a retreat to Jordan and Hermon and Mount Mizar (42:6) sounds far more alluring.

We live in a section of Cookeville, Tennessee, called 'Algood.' There's a non-chain, original type eating place there called the 'Algood Diner.' It's a 1950s sort of place; you seat yourself; most of the clientele is blue collar; construction workers and others come there for their mid-day meal. One can sit at the counter, or at a booth or table. Order from the menu or take what's offered each day at the small buffet. No cloth napkins, no reservations. Every so often when my wife and I want to have our main meal at noon, we traipse over to the Algood Diner. We have plenty to eat, but it's terribly 'plain-jane' and certainly not the first selection you'd make if one were taking a guest to lunch. That's sort of the way the Bible sets things up: if you're after the presence of God, don't surf the internet to pick up some renowned preacher; simply go to public worship. Start there.

Now there is also a *picture* here in this 'appetite' section. The writer likens his longing for God to a deer that 'longs for streams of water' (v. 1). Derek Kidner points out that this is a deer, not a camel, not an animal that can 'tank up' and be impervious to thirst if need be.[3] Perhaps this implies that such longing, such thirst, is an ever *recurring* affair that must be satisfied and satiated again and again. The main question, however, that verses 1-2 pose for us is: Have I such a longing for God? Do I have such a hunger and thirst for His presence? Is such a concept utterly foreign to me? If so, what is wrong?

The writer moves on to focus on his **anguish** (42:3-7). Certain 'contributors' are responsible for this anguish. One is *hostility*. He's driven to repeated tears as he faces the jeers and mockery of those around him: 'all day long they say to me, "Where is your God?"' (v. 3b). We don't know the precise circumstances. But, apparently, some surrounding pagans were asking why his God didn't come to help him in his distress. Why is He leaving you high and dry? Why doesn't He aid you and bring you relief? If your God doesn't 'show up,' what sort of God is He?

Yet the grief from hostility is also aggravated by *memory;* I remember, he says,

> that I used to pass on in the throng,
> how I used to lead them to the house of God
> > with the voice of shouting and praise,
> > a multitude at festival (42:4).

He recalled the thrill and joy of temple worship and his having some degree of leadership in it. But that is gone now and its absence galls him all the more as he faces the

---

3 Derek Kidner, *Psalms 1–72*, TOTC (London: Inter-Varsity, 1973), p. 166.

mockery around him. Sometimes splendid memories can become instruments of depression. That was the case with the seventy-nine-year-old woman who once wrote J. B. Phillips about her trouble. She had cared for her husband who had a series of strokes, then she herself was reduced by paralysis and could no longer assist in parish ministry nor even do ordinary chores. Looking back at all that she lamented:

> [W]here is the dear Christ of experience with whom I have walked and talked through the years? Life is so dreary without him, whereas before it was such a joyous thing! I suppose I shouldn't be bothering about it at seventy-nine—but it seems to matter now more than ever.[4]

'Before it was such a joyous thing!' Sometimes we can remember a 'before,' which is no longer present in the 'now,' doesn't seem recoverable, and it saddens and distresses us.

Then we can say that *locality* may have contributed to the psalmist's trouble. 'My soul,' he says, 'is cast down within me, therefore I remember you' (42:6a). That is a good thing to do when one's soul is in the muck. But then note where this remembering takes place: 'from the land of Jordan and Hermon, from Mount Mizar' (v. 6b). Mount Mizar is a bit of a problem—we've no idea where that was. But it sounds like the writer finds himself east of the Jordan River, near the area of Mt. Hermon, far to the north, maybe some twenty-seven miles west/southwest of Damascus. In short, a long way from 'the house of

---

4 Vera Phillips and Edwin Robertson, *J. B. Phillips: The Wounded Healer* (Grand Rapids: Eerdmans, 1984), p. 84.

God' (v. 4). The problem was not the distance as such but the isolation that the distance imposed. It can still prove a problem in our circumstances. I recently phoned my oldest brother, who is ninety-four, and he mentioned that they had not been able to get to public worship for several weeks. The separation fueled their expectation, hence his anticipation that he could make it this coming Sunday. Naturally, he and his wife can watch a service via the internet, but, as he says, 'It isn't the same.' How much more this problem must aggravate believers who live under repressive regimes (which Yahweh will one day shatter) that prohibit Christians from gathering for any form of group or corporate worship.

All this should be sufficient to explain the psalmist's distress, but he goes on to describe it in terms of *calamity* (42:7):

> Deep keeps calling to deep
>   at the sound of your water-channels
> —all your breakers and your waves
>   have rolled over me.

The word rendered 'water channels' (or waterfalls, NET) occurs only here and in 2 Samuel 5:8, where it is sometimes translated 'water-shaft.' Perhaps the sound of waterfalls conjures up the sea ('deep') and its waves, and he imagines himself overwhelmed under those billows and breakers. He calls them 'your' breakers and 'your' waves—they are ultimately God's, though that is of little comfort to him at the moment. It is sheer calamity; he feels, as we sometimes say, simply smooshed.

I realize that one does not analyze intense poetical expression in cold, rational terms. Still, it's interesting to note that the psalmist takes both time and thought to detail what it is that stirs up his misery. Hostility, memory, locality, and even calamity all seem to contribute to it. He expresses it vigorously, but he has had to think it out, almost to itemize it, in order to do that. Sometimes, when I take my vehicle into the auto shop, I go with a typed list. At the top is my name, phone number (though I usually wait on it), and year and make of my vehicle. I might put down a conventional oil and filter change, rotating the tires (tyres!), checking the status of my brakes (in need of replacement?), and changing the air filter. I write them down in 1-2-3-4 order. The service manager often seems to appreciate this—he simply asks if he can keep the paper and staples it to the work order. I do this so that I can be reasonably sure everything will be attended to. I put it all down. It seems to me that that is what the psalmist (as well as other psalm writers) does with his anguish: he itemizes it before God from several different angles. It's intense, it's emotional, but he *had to think it through* in order to express it in such detail. And these biblical 'lamenters' seem to sense they have a God who welcomes hearing their complaint in all its detail. Why tell such multi-sided anguish unless we assume we have an incredibly interested and merciful God?

Then, thirdly, in 42:8-10 we seem to meet with a bit of **alleviation**. That is, our psalmist implies that it is not all totally dark in his trial. There are shafts, or maybe just slivers, of light in the midst of it all. Here he is in this trouble and yet 'by day Yahweh commands his unfailing love and at night his song is with me' (42:8). Interesting that in a series of psalms that normally uses 'God' of Israel's deity, here our writer uses the covenant name,

Yahweh. And his 'unfailing love' is *ḥesed*, Yahweh's love that sticks and holds and refuses to let go. So he is not totally bereft of comfort either by day or by night.

Though we may be pardoned for wondering! I say that because in the last of verse 8 he expands on what 'his [Yahweh's] song' is—he calls it a 'prayer to the God of my life.' Then in verses 9-10 he tells us what that night-time prayer is:[5]

> 'Why have you forgotten me?
> Why do I go round mourning
> because the enemy presses me down?
> It's like crushing my bones
>   when my foes mock me,
>   when they say to me all day long,
>   "Where is your God?"'

We may wonder if one could really call that prayer a 'song' (v. 8)! It seems simply to repeat his despair. And yet. Notice it is not entirely without hope: he prefaces his song/prayer with, 'I say to God, *my rock*' (v. 9a). Even though, however, his prayer still seems to focus on his trouble, he is praying to his 'rock' and to the Lord who mixes His 'unfailing love' with His breakers and waves (v. 7). There's a clear hint of hope blended into his discouragement.

During the American Revolutionary War, the colonists' hopes were pretty much dashed late in 1776. But on Christmas night, General Washington got 2,400 troops across the

---

5   Quotation marks in our English versions are supplied by trans-lators. Almost without exception these versions close off the 'quote' of the prayer at the end of verse 9. But I think this is wrong—the prayer takes in both verses 9 and 10. Cf. Allen Ross, *A Commentary on the Psalms,* 3 vols. (Grand Rapids: Kregel, 2013), 2:26.

Delaware River, marching on icy roads, so that at 8:00 a.m. on December 26 they could attack the British garrison at Trenton (New Jersey) manned by German mercenaries, some of whom had celebrated intensely the night before. An hour of fighting and the Americans had bagged nearly 900 prisoners, while over 100 of the enemy were eliminated. The British sent Cornwallis to deal with this reverse. He came to Trenton, leaving an outpost of 1,200 men at Princeton in the north. Washington slithered away from the Trenton area by night, and attacked and defeated Cornwallis' remnant at Princeton. The news of these victories, limited as they were, had an 'electric effect' on the morale of the colonists.[6] The war would continue; many troubles lay ahead. But, in the middle of despair, there were these two small victories that put fresh heart into the Americans.

The psalm implies that Yahweh sometimes deals with His people like that. He gives them a kind of interim relief, some small token in the middle of trouble that keeps their hope alive. We are cast down but He makes us sense His *ḥesed* and, though our prayers still bemoan our troubles, we are convinced that we are nevertheless speaking to 'God our rock.'

Then, particularly when we come to 43:1-5, we sense there is an air of **anticipation** in the psalm(s). In all of 42 we meet description and lament, but in 43 we hear the first 'positive' petitions:

'Give me justice…'
'Plead my case…'
'Rescue me …' (v. 1).

---

6   Thomas Fleming, *Liberty! The American Revolution* (New York: Viking, 1997), pp. 217-24.

Then we read the basis for such petitions: 'for you are my fortress-God' (v. 2a).[7]

The 'whys' are still there (43:2b), but one feels a sliver of light sneaking through the cracks in 43:3-4. He asks God to send His two 'agents,' Light and Truth, to conduct him back to familiar turf:

> **They** can lead me;
> let them bring me to your holy hill
>   and to your dwelling-place!
> Then I will come to the altar of God,
>   to God, my exceeding joy.

He wants to be back in Jerusalem, in Zion, in the temple. But the build-up to the climax must not be missed: holy hill, dwelling-place, altar, then 'to God, my exceeding joy'!

Let's pause to pass on a kind of parable of our text. It was May of 1843. The General Assembly of the Church of Scotland was meeting in St. Andrew's Church, Edinburgh. However, after opening prayer, the past moderator did not constitute the Assembly but read a protest against the government's domineering control of the church. He then walked out, joined by something like 450 ministers, who were willing to leave their salaries and manses, if need be. It was the 'Disruption,' the formation of the Free Church of Scotland. According to the account, the protesting ministers went down the hill from the church and assembled in Tanfield Hall. A heavy thunder-cloud presided over the streets, and the hall was so dark one could scarcely make out individual figures. But Dr.

---

7   Here I have stolen Alec Motyer's delightful rendering; *Psalms by the Day* (Ross-shire: Christian Focus, 2016), p. 112. By this time, it should also be obvious that I treat Psalms 42 and 43 as a combined unit.

Chalmers rose and gave out the psalm. It was the forty-third. He began with the line, 'O send thy light forth and thy truth.' At those words the sun escaped from behind the clouds and shone through the windows.[8] Whatever one makes of it, that is the sort of 'breakthrough' our psalmist seems to expect.

But another pause. Note what, above all, he expects:

Then I will come to the altar of God,
to God, my exceeding joy (v. 4a).

I love and have retained the happy rendering of the AV/KJV: 'my exceeding joy.' That statement both thrills me and condemns me. Far above places and circumstances and troubles, God Himself is my exceeding joy, my only prize. And yet how seldom do I think like that! This exclamation by an Old Testament believer rivals anything you will find in Philippians 3.

Back to this matter of anticipation. You may think my seeing hints of a change in 43:1-5 are too subjective. We can't go on 'sense' and 'feelings,' you say. But you cannot evade the tenacity that pervades these psalms in the refrain:

Hope in God,
for I will yet praise him
(42:5, 11; 43:5).

Amid the longing 'when?' of 42:2, the mocking 'wheres?' of 42:3 and 10, and the anguished 'whys?' of 42:9 and 43:2,

---

8   John Ker, *The Psalms in History and Biography* (reprint ed., Birmingham, AL: Solid Ground Christian Books, 2006), pp. 73-74; cf. Norman L. Walker, *Chapters from the History of the Free Church of Scotland* (Edinburgh: Oliphant, Anderson & Ferrier, 1895), pp. 17-19.

there is simply this rock-ribbed certainty that, somehow, all will be well. 'I *will* yet praise him.' His anticipation stares you in the face in that refrain. Which suggests that there is always a bottom in our pit of despair. Each of these refrains consists of the psalmist addressing himself ('Why are you cast down, *my soul?*'). Martyn Lloyd-Jones in his classic *Spiritual Depression* argues that troubles tend to overwhelm you because 'you are listening to yourself instead of talking to yourself.'[9] In these refrains, the writer keeps talking to himself—and the non-negotiable certainty he keeps repeating keeps his chin above water.

---

9   D. Martyn Lloyd-Jones, *Spiritual Depression: Its Causes and Cure* (Grand Rapids: Eerdmans, 1965), p. 20.

Psalm 44

To the music leader. Belonging to the sons of Korah. A maskil.

(1) O God, we have heard with our ears,
        our fathers have told us
            the work you worked in their days,
                in days long ago.

(2) You, your hand drove out nations,
        but you planted them;
        you brought disaster on the peoples
        but you set them free.

(3) No, it was not by their sword that they possessed the land;
        nor was it their arm that saved them,
        but your right hand and your arm and the light of your face,
        because you showed favor to them.

(4) You are the one, my King, O God;
        command victories for Jacob!

(5) By your help we knock down our foes,
        in your name we trample those who rise against us.

(6) For it is not in my bow that I trust,
        and my sword will not save me;

(7) but you have saved us from our foes,
        and you have put to shame those who hate us.

(8) **In God** we have boasted all day long,
        and it is your name we will praise forever. Selah.

(9) Yet you have cast us off, so that you brought us to disgrace;
and you do not go out with our armies.

(10) You make us turn backward from the foe
and those who hate us have plundered us.

(11) You give us up like sheep to be devoured
and among the nations you have scattered us.

(12) You sell your people at no cost,
and you have not made a profit with their market price.

(13) You make us the scorn of our neighbors,
something to mock and scoff at to those around us.

(14) You make us a wisecrack among the nations,
a laughing-stock among the peoples.

(15) All day long my disgrace is before me,
and shame has covered me,

(16) because of the voice of scorn and cut-downs,
because of the presence of the enemy
and the one taking revenge.

(17) All this has come upon us,
yet we have not forgotten you,
and we have not been false to your covenant.

(18) Our heart has not turned back,
so that our steps turned aside from your way.

(19) But you have crushed us in the place of jackals
and covered us with deep darkness.

(20) If we had forgotten the name of our God,
so that we spread out our hands to a strange god,

(21) would not God search this out,
for he knows the secrets of the heart?

(22) No, it is on your account that we have been killed
all day long,
counted as sheep for slaughtering.

(23) Arise! Why do you sleep, O Lord?
      Wake up—don't cast (us) off forever!

(24) Why do you hide your face?
      Why do you forget our miseries and oppression?

(25) For our soul has sunk down to the dust,
      our belly has clung to the earth.

(26) Rise up, bring help to us!
      And redeem us on account of your unfailing love.

6
WHEN THEOLOGY DOESN'T WORK

Gary Larson has been known for his 'Far Side' cartoons, rather 'whacko' pieces of imagination that sometimes make one think.[1] One of his offerings depicts the scene outside 'J & J Stockyards' where a number of cattle are milling about with rather blank but contented expressions. One, however, that has what looks like a large tumor across her head, wears a rather foreboding and anxious look. The blurb beneath the cartoon reads: 'Only Claire, with her oversized brain, wore an expression of concern.' Claire is different from all the rest. She seemed to sense what usually happened at stockyards. Psalm 44 is like Claire. It's a bit different from other psalms. Oh, like a number of them, it's a lament. Not an individual lament but a 'congregational' lament. One in which the corporate

---

1   There's an irreverent strain in some of Larson's work; selecting a sample does not imply endorsement of the whole.

body of believers complains of God's ways. In this psalm, however, Yahweh's people complain that though they have been faithful to Yahweh, He has nevertheless cast them off and refused to bless and keep them. Why, they say, does Yahweh meet fidelity with disaster? It's as if they conclude that the theology they've learned (cf. vv. 1-8) doesn't work. It's a bit different. Let's try to trace the path of their faith through the psalm.

The psalm begins by underscoring **the continuity of faith** (vv. 1-8), and the people, the congregation, the 'we' of verse 1, speak first of the *basis* for that faith (vv. 1-3). It all started with what 'our fathers have told us' (v. 1) of God's deeds in past days. There was their testimony, especially about the 'conquest' (v. 2) when Yahweh drove out nations and planted His people in Canaan (see the book of Joshua). And that could not/cannot be chalked up to their skill or power—it was 'your right hand and your arm and the light of your face' (v. 3) that gave this success. Not of works lest anyone should boast. The message in their testimony focuses on the sufficiency of God.

The whole Bible story, of course, points to this, even though here in the psalm the conquest is primarily in view. But go back over the story. Think of the patriarchs (Gen. 12–50), of their touch-and-go existence in Canaan and elsewhere; see how God protects the fragile. Go to Egypt, consider Israel in her bondage and see how God delivers the slaves (Exod. 1–15). Follow them in those long years in the trackless wilderness and watch how God provides for the needy (e.g., Exod. 16–17; Deut. 2:7). Then they enter the land (Joshua) and you see how God overpowers obstacles, whether rivers or fortresses or their own folly (Josh. 9) or coalitions massed against them

(Josh. 10–11). You can follow this (pitiful) people right into exile (2 Kings 24–25) and yet see how God revives the hopeless (e.g., Ezra 1:1-4; Jer. 29:1-11). Go on and stand at the crucifixion and see how God tramples death and sin. It's always the sufficiency of God. 'Not by their sword ... nor was it their arm that saved them' (v. 3).

Then, in verses 4-8, the congregation reveals the impact of what 'our fathers have told us.' It is not a matter of 'they' but also of 'we.' They are saying, We have found this God to be the same toward us, and so they confess:

> By your help we knock down our foes,
> in your name we trample those who rise against us.
> For it's not in my bow that I trust,
> and my sword will not save me;
> but you have saved us from our foes ... (vv. 5-7a).

The testimony of the fathers is not merely 'the old, old story,' but 'this is *my* story, this is *my* song,' they say.[2] So this later generation takes up the same faith as a previous generation had passed on to them. 'Our fathers have told us' (v. 1). Yes, how shall they hear without a parent? What a beautiful thing to see—a later generation still holding to the faith of their forebears. Theirs is not merely a historical faith but a contemporary faith—in an all-sufficient God.

Here, I cannot help but think of an anecdote sent in to *Reader's Digest* by one of its readers. She said that one of their local elementary school teachers was showing a copy of the Declaration of Independence to her class. It went from desk to desk and finally came to Luigi, a first-generation American. The lad studied the document

---

2   Cf. the refrain to 'Blessed Assurance,' *Trinity Hymnal* (1990), No. 693.

reverently and then, before passing it along, solemnly added his own signature to those already on the document. Isn't that what we need to press upon those we sometimes call 'covenant children,' young teens, for example, who have been taught the faith and raised in the faith—but they need to solemnly add their own signature.

All well and good, but now, in verses 9-22, we meet **the dilemma of faith**. It seems to begin in *contradiction* (vv. 9-16); it's as if the gear-shift has been slammed into reverse:

> Yet you have cast us off, so that you brought us
>   to disgrace;
> and you do not go out with our armies.
> You make us turn backward from the foe
> and those who hate us have plundered us.
> You give us up like sheep to be devoured
> and among the nations you have scattered us.
> You sell your people at no cost,
> and you have not made a profit with their market
>   price (vv. 9-12).

'Yet you have cast us off....' The new hard facts of experience on the battlefield contradict the truth we have believed—and experienced (vv. 5, 7-8). So now we know all about flight, plundering, death, exile, and slavery. And to aggravate it all, we hear the mockery and derision of the pagans around us (vv. 13-16). We're a 'laughing-stock among the peoples' (v. 13). Imagine the sort of ditties Israel may have faced:

> See how those Israelites run when we face them
>   in battle,
> when we simply shoot some arrows and let our
>   swords rattle.

What joy to burst through them like a flood
and spill all their so-called covenantal blood.
Their faith in Yahweh has hit a terrible snag,
for he can't seem to fight his way out of a wet
    paper bag.

Shame for them, but shame for Yahweh as well.

You can feel the contradiction in brief by simply putting verses 7a and 9a side by side: 'You have saved us,' 'yet you have cast us off.' It's the problem of experience versus creed, or perhaps of later experience versus previous experience. Let's stop a moment simply to say that the Bible recognizes the problem—the Bible itself raises the problem to get you to face it. It's not as though an unexpected death occurs and you say, 'If God really loves me, then how can He…?' No, no. That reaction just shows you haven't spent much time reading the prayers of God's people (the Psalms), because then you will see that *the Bible forces this problem upon you*. It's trying to get you to think about this anomaly, hopefully ahead of time.

Wycliffe translators have related that a Gahuku tribesman of New Guinea who is confused or baffled over something and doesn't know what to believe about it all may say that he 'heard his two ears.' Which meant that one ear was telling him one thing and the other ear was telling him something else, and he didn't know which one to believe.[3] So in this psalm the Lord's people seem to be 'hearing their two ears.'

But there's a further aggravation to this contradiction of experience. There seems to be no apparent

---

3   *Searchlight on Bible Words* (Huntington Beach, CA: Wycliffe Bible Translators, 1972), p. 76.

reason or explanation for these reverses they've endured. In verses 17-21 it's as if they say: If we had turned away from the Lord, thumbing our noses at His commands and cuddling up to some other gods, then we could understand His bringing the covenant curses (cf. Lev. 26, Deut. 28) down on us. But that, they claim, is not the case:

> All this has come upon us,
> yet we have not forgotten you,
> and we have not been false to your covenant.
> Our heart has not turned back,
> so that our steps turned aside from your way.
> But you have crushed us in the place of jackals
> ... (vv. 17-19a).

They are not claiming sinlessness, but general covenant first-commandment-like fidelity. Of course, after one reads through 1–2 Kings, one wonders just when the nation could make a claim like this! But there must have been a window of a generation when they could. There has been covenant fidelity, they say, but no covenant blessing. 'Yahweh will make your enemies who rise up against you to be stricken down before you; they will come out in one way against you but will flee in seven ways before you' (Deut. 28:7; cf. Lev. 26:7-8). But there has been none of that. Quite the reverse. 'You have crushed us' (v. 19a). Theology doesn't work.

Yet there may be a sliver of light on this dilemma. It's in verse 22:

> No, it is on your account that we have been killed
> all day long,
> counted as sheep for slaughtering.

As Derek Kidner notes, the psalmist doesn't flesh out the matter, but it is here. What's here? 'The revolutionary thought that suffering may be a battle-scar rather than a punishment; the price of loyalty in a world which is at war with God.'[4] The opening phrase of verse 22 can be construed a couple of ways. If we translate, 'Because of you,' it could mean: 'You have done it for whatever mysterious reason.' Or we can translate, 'On your account,' that is, 'for your sake,' which carries the idea 'because we are your people and hated because of that.' I think the latter alternative is better—the same Hebrew phrase seems to have this sense in Psalm 69:7 (v. 8 in Heb.) and Jeremiah 15:15.

It's John 15:18-19 ahead of time. I've just read of folks in Chan Thar, a Christian village in Myanmar, whose homes were destroyed by the Myanmar military. It came under fire, then soldiers went house to house igniting them. Over 300 homes burned down. All 350 homes in another Christian village were also destroyed. 'On your account'—because Buddhists hate Christians. Go to Nigeria and hear the mourners in Zion as they carry Jesus' disciples to their graves, gunned down because Islamic terrorists hate Christians.

You know, of course, that Paul quotes this verse in Romans 8:36, part of that defiant crescendo of assurance in the last of Romans 8. What's so interesting is the way Paul 'sandwiches' his quote of Psalm 44:22. Preceding it, he cries, 'Who shall separate us from the love of Christ? Affliction or distress or persecution or famine or nakedness or peril or sword?' (v. 35). And following

---

4   Derek Kidner, *Psalms 1–72,* TOTC (London: Inter-Varsity, 1973), p. 170.

our verse, he exclaims, 'No, in all these things we are super-conquerors through him who loved us' (v. 37). He takes our verse, affirms its reality, and yet places it in the middle of inseparable love.

Inseparable love and severe suffering. What a combination. It reminds me of theologian Helmut Thielicke telling of his quest to protest and reverse his dismissal from his university lectureship by the Nazi regime. He went to the den of Naziism, the Brown House in Munich. He was having no success, but a young civil servant was there, one of the few civilians present, who happened to fix his eye on Thielicke. He probably appeared lost and helpless. The fellow asked if he could be of assistance. After a few questions, Thielicke poured out his whole dilemma to the young fellow and the latter suggested a pecking order of officials they might try. In the end it proved futile, but what staggered Thielicke was finding such kind, courteous, attentive assistance in that nefarious den of thugs.[5] Kindness and Naziism! That is something like what Paul does. He takes the sad scourge inflicted on God's people and wraps it in the assurance of inseparable love. We do well in our dark days, and always, to remember the 'unusual' combination.

Finally, note that the psalm closes with **the plea of faith** (vv. 23-26). But it is faith that is *accusing* (vv. 23-24):

Arise! Why do you sleep, O Lord?
Wake up—don't cast (us) off forever!
Why do you hide your face?
Why do you forget our miseries and oppression?

---

5 Helmut Thielicke, *Notes from a Wayfarer* (New York: Paragon House, 1995), pp. 116-17.

The pray-ers are driven near distraction. They imply the Lord acts like pagan deities, who sleep and take their rest and 'zone out.' It's shocking language and yet it is the sort of speech God allows us to use in our despair. It's the way the disciples accused Jesus: 'Teacher, don't you care that we are perishing?' (Mark 4:38). That can frequently be the case: that we are in some degree of perishing and Jesus is asleep in the boat. Sometimes, faith breaks out in accusation—it is the anguish over the 'absence' of God.

And yet this is a faith that is *clinging*. 'Rise up, bring help to us! And redeem us on account of your unfailing love' (v. 26). Well, matters are still desperate, but the psalmist plays his trump card. 'Unfailing love' is *ḥesed*. That's love but more; it's loyal love, steadfast love, committed love, love that will not let go, love with stick-um on it, with crazy glue all over it. And if that's the way Yahweh is (Exod. 34:6), then all is not hopeless.

But perhaps the premier idea here is that faith is *persisting*. That's what is most striking about verses 23-26. The psalm does not end like a nicely-packaged half-hour TV drama with all in place at the end. The threads of agony are still unraveled and cluttering the floor at the end of the psalm. What does faith do in such a situation? It keeps crying to the God who has not heard—there is nowhere else to go. It's called monotheism.

Psalm 45

To the music leader. Upon 'Lilies.' For the sons of Korah.
A maskil. A love song.

(1) My heart overflows with a splendid theme;
    I say, 'My work is about a king,'
    my tongue is the pen of a skilled scribe.

(2) You are far more handsome than the sons of men;
    grace has been poured upon your lips;
    clearly, God has blessed you forever.

(3) Strap your sword on your thigh, O warrior!
    Your splendor and your majesty!

(4) And in your majesty ride on successfully
        for the cause of truth and humility-righteousness,
    and let your right hand teach you fearful things.

(5) Your sharpened arrows
        —peoples fall under you—
    in the heart of the king's enemies.

(6) Your throne, O God, [is] forever and ever,
    a scepter of uprightness [is] the scepter of your kingdom

(7) You have loved righteousness
        and you have hated wickedness,
    therefore, God, your God, has anointed you
        with the oil of gladness more than your companions.

(8) All your robes [exude] myrrh and aloes and cassia,
     from ivory palaces music has made you rejoice.

(9) The daughters of kings are among those you esteem;
     the queen stands at your right hand in gold from Ophir.

(10) Listen, O daughter, and see and turn your ear [to me],
     and forget your people and your father's house

(11) and let the king desire your beauty,
     for he is your sovereign
     and you must show obeisance to him.

(12) And [there is] the daughter of Tyre with a gift!
     The richest of people will seek your favor.

(13) How totally glorious—the king's daughter in the inner chamber!
     Her clothing plaited with gold!

(14) In multi-colored attire she is led to the king,
     young women, her companions, following her,
        are brought to you.

(15) They are led with gladness and joy,
     they are brought into the palace of the king.

(16) In place of your fathers there will be your sons
     —you will appoint them princes throughout all the earth.

(17) I will cause your name to be remembered
        down through all generations;
     therefore peoples will praise you
        forever and ever.

7

A LOVE SONG CAN BE A BIT OF TROUBLE

It was a sensational feat and cause for massive celebrations when Atlanta Braves' outfielder, Henry Aaron, broke Babe Ruth's 714 home run record in the early 1970s. But it had its 'down' side. There were, naturally, extreme pressures Aaron faced, but worst of all was the vicious, racially-driven hate mail that came because Aaron was black. A superb achievement but terrible difficulties. I don't want to over-dramatize a matter of biblical interpretation, but, at least in principle, Psalm 45 is like that. Here is a magnificent piece depicting a resplendent occasion but which generates head-scratchers and debates among interpreters. It is billed 'a love song' and seems to portray a royal marriage. The description of the king (vv. 2-9) seems so ideal, beyond the historical, that one might imagine it is describing the messianic figure. But the queen (vv. 9b-11) soon brings us down to earth. Unless one is going to idealize the queen as a cipher for the people of God, one cannot take the psalm this way. Sounds like we have to do with a real woman.

If, according to a popular view, the psalm's setting is a wedding between a king of Israel or Judah with a royal princess, then one becomes totally frustrated with pin-pointing a particular historical moment. Most of Israel or Judah's historical kings hardly come close to fitting the royal resume of this psalm, not without swallowing a camel or two anyway. Then there are verses 6-7, where the psalm seems to address the king as 'God,' which causes some interpreters to reach for their translator's bag of tricks. And Hebrews 1 seems to take it all in stride.

The way to get around such difficulties is to write a work on 'Some of My Favorite Psalms,' where one can be selective. But if one is taking a chunk of Psalms and therefore each psalm as it comes—well, then, here is Psalm 45 and we have to face it. The general structure of the psalm is fairly clear: verses 1-9 address and describe the king, verses 10-15 the queen, and verses 16-17 address the king again. So we plunge in, sure to make someone somewhere unhappy with some of our conclusions.

In the first segment, we are told of **a king to rave about** (vv. 1-9). The psalmist tells us he is 'keyed up' over his subject matter (v. 1) and launches into his description of the king by highlighting *his obvious appeal:* 'You are far more handsome than the sons of men; grace has been poured upon your lips' (v. 2a). He then describes the king as 'warrior' and *his military success* (vv. 3-5). He is to sally forth with sword and splendor and press home 'the cause of truth and humility-righteousness' (v. 4b).[1] McCann reminds us that 'righteousness' elsewhere 'appears in association with God's reign to designate God's will for the world' (e.g., Pss. 9:8; 96:13; 97:2; 98:9).[2] So here we should take it broadly, we might say, of how God will 'put things right' at the last. This is part of the king's cause. This success is no cushion-and-hand-cream affair; rather, the king's arrows drop his enemies in their tracks (v. 5).

Our writer goes on to laud *his righteous character* (vv. 6-7). We will come back to verse 6a, but note that the king's royal scepter is a scepter of 'uprightness' and that he has strong but godly passions: 'you have loved righteousness and you have hated wickedness' (v. 7a). There are paltry few of Israel or Judah's historical kings of whom that could be said. Finally, he recounts *his impressive splendor* (vv. 8-9) with its fragrance, music, attendants— and the queen.

We go back now to verses 6-7. It is one thing for a writer to address a king in somewhat hyperbolic fashion, but what is one to do when the writer says, 'Your throne, O God, [is] forever and ever'? That is the real 'kicker' in this psalm. In Egypt the king was thought to be divine — but not in Israel. And yet here.... So, it seems there was a scholarly scurry (on display in some translations) to avoid what the text seemed to say. The NEB offers 'Your throne

---

1   That is the Hebrew text, a sort of hyphenated idea: humility-righteousness, perhaps best explained by Alexander as 'right asserted in humility against a wrong maintained by pride and selfishness' (J. A. Alexander, *The Psalms: Translated and Explained* [reprint ed., Grand Rapids: Zondervan, n.d.], p. 203).

2   J. Clinton McCann, Jr., 'The Book of Psalms,' NIB, 12 vols. (Nashville: Abingdon, 1996), 4:861.

is like God's throne, eternal' (RSV similar), without so much as a note that there are alternative possibilities. Or, changing vowels and doing a little body-English one comes up with 'God has enthroned you for all eternity' (REB). But the simplest and most straight-forward is that in my translation. The pre-Christian Septuagint took it this way, and even the NRSV does so (which has no penchant for agreeing with the angels).[3]

So how are we to look at this? Some may point out that occasionally in the Old Testament we find 'gods' (*Elohim*) being used of judges and kings (e.g., perhaps Exod. 21:6; Ps. 82:1, 6). However, E. W. Hengstenberg pointed out that nowhere is *any single magistrate* called *Elohim* (God, gods) but only the *magistracy* as representing the tribunal of God.[4] So it looks like we have the king addressed as 'God.'

---

3   Part of the rub readers feel is that in verse 6 the psalm addresses the king as 'God,' but then in verse 7 (still speaking to the king) says, 'God, your God, has anointed you.' So he is called 'God' and then we hear that God is his God. Derek Kidner notes, 'This paradox is consistent with the incarnation, but mystifying in any other context. It is an example of Old Testament language bursting its banks, to demand a more than human fulfillment' (*Psalms 1–72*, TOTC [London: Inter-Varsity, 1973], p. 172). For an assessment of the whole matter, one can check Murray J. Harris, 'The Translation of *Elohim* in Psalm 45:7-8,' *Tyndale Bulletin* 35 (1984): 65-89. In NT usage Hebrews 1:8-9 quotes Psalm 45:6-7. After the introductory 'confession' (1:1-4), the writer of Hebrews sets out two opening sections: (1) the supremacy of the Son's position, 1:5-14; and (2) the urgency of the Son's proclamation, 2:1-4. In the former section, he argues that the Son is superior to angels in that He has a superior name (vv. 4b-5), a superior homage (vv. 6-7), a superior address (vv. 8-12), and a superior destiny (v. 13). There is no doubt how Hebrews takes Psalm 45:6.

4   As noted in Walter C. Kaiser, Jr., *The Messiah in the Old Testament* (Grand Rapids: Zondervan, 1995), p. 129n.

The Old Testament does ascribe deity to the coming messianic figure, a matter too often downplayed. In Isaiah 9:6 he is called 'mighty God.'[5] He is not only the shoot *from* Jesse but the 'root *of* Jesse' (Isa. 11:1, 10). Often overlooked, I think, is Isaiah 50:10, where 'obeying the voice of his [Yahweh's] servant' is on a level with 'fearing Yahweh,' and hence suggestive of the deity of the Servant. Without long discussion, David seems to call the Messiah 'my Lord' in Psalm 110:1. Then there is that mysterious grammatical switch in Zechariah 12:10, where Yahweh is speaking, 'And they shall look on *me* whom they have pierced, and they shall mourn over *him*' (emphasis mine). There is some sort of identity between the 'me' and the 'him.' Or there is the 'one like a son of man' in Daniel 7, who is clearly a human but also a *divine* figure, since 'all peoples, nations, and languages' are to 'serve' Him (v. 14). The Aramaic verb for 'serve' (*pelaḥ*) is used nine times in the book of Daniel and always of 'serving' or paying reverence to deity or a purported deity. So the NIV translates it as 'worship.'[6] These are a few indicators that in Old Testament theology the coming messianic king was indeed a divine figure, and, if that is so, should we be quite so non-plussed should a psalmist share the same view? The problem may be with us: it is totally unexpected; we just don't think anyone would say this.

In my files, I have copies of my father's annual reports which he gave to churches he served as pastor. At the

---

5   This cannot be toned down to 'God-like hero'; see my *Stump Kingdom* (Ross-shire: Christian Focus, 2017), p. 68.
6   See my *The Message of Daniel*, Bible Speaks Today (Nottingham: Inter-Varsity, 2013), p. 100.

end of each year, he would type up a one-page summary of his ministry for the year in question. A good bit of it was statistical, with a few comments about the church or his ministry. Let's take the report for 1956. Near the end of the report, he included a little squib that during the year he had received invitations from two other churches in the neighboring state to consider coming as their pastor. He then indicated that 'family conditions' at the moment dictated that those invitations had to be refused, 'although,' he wrote, 'they offered nice increases in salary.' Now you simply don't expect to hear a brash comment like that in a pastor's report. It's too blatant and suggestive, and blunt. But that was my father. He never felt he had to stay crammed within the bounds of conventional propriety. He said it, shocking as it was, and got away with it.

Perhaps that's the case with Psalm 45. Nor should we necessarily be so surprised. The writer has already told us that he is simply bubbling over with his theme (v. 1); he is clearly 'taken' with the king. Should we then be too amazed if he bursts the bounds of 'propriety' in verse 6 as he perhaps takes into view the ultimate King to come? The real problem may be: why are *we* not so fascinated with this king?

The psalm, however, is not totally about the king— the queen stands beside him (v. 9b). Hard to avoid, then, thinking that the psalm involves a real royal wedding. So in the second segment we meet **a queen to advise and admire** (vv. 10-15), where our psalmist speaks of her duty (vv. 10-11), her recognition (v. 12), and her splendor (vv. 13-15).

He begins with his advice and that about her duty:

Listen, O daughter, and see and turn your ear [to me],
and forget your people and your father's house
and let the king desire your beauty,
for he is your sovereign
and you must show obeisance to him (vv. 10-11).

Of course, that's enough for even a moderate modern feminist to swallow her chewing gum! And that is what is so refreshing about the Bible—it never kowtows to the settled shibboleths of current fashionable opinion. But such folks may well go running from Psalm 45 screaming, 'Patriarchal!' and alleging that the queen is told to become a doormat for male domination. That's over-reaction. But the queen *is* told she has a new loyalty and so she should 'forget the things that are behind' (cf. v. 10b) and submit herself to the king (v. 11), 'for he is your sovereign.' But she hardly looks miserable as she stands next to the king decked out in the finest gold jewels (v. 9b).

And who is that just a bit off to the side? It's a 'daughter of Tyre'—with a gift no less (v. 12)! Princesses and representatives from other peoples have arrived to offer recognition to the queen, simply because she belongs to Israel's king. But the bulk of the psalmist's description focuses on the sheer splendor of it all (vv. 13-15), especially here of the queen. 'How totally glorious' (v. 13a) she is, dazzling in robes and clothes laced with gold (v. 13b), processing in kaleidoscopic splendor with her ladies-in-waiting and joyfully entering the king's palace (vv. 14-15). Jaws doubtless drop at the sumptuous scene. Our writer is simply 'taken' with it all.

Many of us, I suppose, are rather cynical about such lavish displays. We tend to be suspicious of celebrations and displays of enthusiasm. But, oh, it's so good to see a bit of it sometimes. It's a long way from a royal wedding, but let me give you a small sample. My wife and I had to travel to North Carolina for a family funeral recently. It was on a weekend, so we made a point of attending church in the area on Sunday morning. A former student was pastor of the church. The preaching was so refreshing, and not just because of the matter but because of the manner. He projected his voice and spoke out—no one would have trouble hearing—and he spoke with animation and liveliness and, well, gusto. It was not 'over the top,' but he preached with enthusiasm and one sensed that what he said really mattered. Perhaps it stood out because, sadly, much preaching is not like that.

So don't turn up your nose when you hear our psalmist waxing ecstatic over the splendor of the king (vv. 2, 8-9) and queen (vv. 13-15). The king is at least one of David's royal line (cf. 2 Sam. 7:12-16) from which the Messiah eventually comes. So in one sense the writer's enthusiasm over this royal wedding is really enthusiasm over the coming of the kingdom of God, and, by implication, over the final descendant of that line, Jesus our Lord. And Paul tells us that if our heads are screwed on straight, we can't help but become ecstatic over 'the surpassing worth' of knowing Jesus our Lord (Phil. 3:8)—something more precious than the gold of Ophir.

Finally, in the last two verses (vv. 16-17) the psalmist speaks of **a future to long for**. Here the Hebrew text uses masculine pronouns and verb forms—hence the writer is addressing the king again. Here he so much as says that he has not only celebrated a royal marriage but that he also anticipates an ongoing kingdom. If the king appoints his sons as 'princes throughout all the earth'

(v. 16), that certainly implies the pervasiveness of his regime. Should we press the scope of 'throughout *all* the earth'? And our psalmist is convinced his song will make the king simply unforgettable, 'down through all generations' (v. 17a), and so 'peoples will praise [him] forever and ever' (v. 17b). Whatever one makes of verses 16-17 in detail, they say that the king will have a continuing kingdom and that he will be remembered and delighted in for all time.

Some may quibble about the language in these verses, perhaps considering 'all the earth,' 'all generations,' and 'forever and ever' as so much courtly hyperbole. But what if it's not? What if it's a quasi-prophecy of what is to come? Does it claim too much? Is it too fantastic?

Andrew Roberts, recent biographer of Churchill, relates how Churchill once predicted to a friend that 'great upheavals, terrible struggles' and unimaginable wars would come, that London would be attacked, that Churchill himself would be eminent in its defense. Somehow, he averred, Britain would be subject to a 'tremendous invasion' and Churchill would be in command of London's defenses and would save London and England from such disaster. He stressed that London would be in danger and that he, because of his high office, would find himself saving the capital and Empire. The fascinating fact is that such claims were not expressed anywhere near 1940, but in 1891, when Churchill was sixteen years old![7] If even human 'predictions,' unreal as they may seem, can prove accurate, we should be cautious

---

7   Andrew Roberts, *Churchill: Walking with Destiny* (New York: Viking, 2018), p. 975.

with biblical poetry before we toss it into the dust-bin of overcooked hyperbole. No, there is more than a royal wedding here; there is a continuing kingdom—and we, no less than the queen, must submit to this King.

One more thing. Perhaps we stretch language too far, but the last of verse 17 ought to be pondered: 'therefore peoples will praise you forever and ever.' McCann says, 'Ordinarily, praise is reserved for God....'[8] Might this be a hint that the writer was not confining his king-description to a merely human king? Is he perhaps telling us that verse 6 was *not* a slip of the pen?

---

8   McCann, 4:862.

Psalm 46

To the music leader. Belonging to the sons of Korah.
Upon Alamoth. A song.

(1) God is our refuge and strength,
      a well-proved help in troubles.

(2) Therefore, we are not going to fear
      when the earth changes,
      when the mountains topple into the heart of the seas!

(3) Let its waters roar, let them foam!
      Let the mountains tremble in its raging! Selah.

(4) A river! Its streams make glad the city of God,
      the holy dwelling of the Most High.

(5) God is in the midst of her; she will not topple;
      God will help her when morning breaks.

(6) Nations have roared! Kingdoms have toppled!
      He has thundered with his voice—the earth melts!

(7) Yahweh of hosts is with us;
      the God of Jacob is our high fortress. Selah.

(8) Come, look at the works of Yahweh,
      the desolations he has made in the earth,

(9) causing wars to stop to the end of the earth!
      He shatters the bow;
      he snaps the spear;
      he burns the battle-wagons in the fire!

(10) 'Stop it! And know that I am God;
     I will be exalted among the nations,
     I will be exalted throughout the earth!'

(11) Yahweh of hosts is with us;
     the God of Jacob is our high fortress. Selah.

8

The City of God in a Crumbling World

One of the men in Martyn Lloyd-Jones' congregation depicted his spiritual odyssey with three pictures he had placed on his mantelpiece. One, taken by a former friend, showed him helplessly inebriated, leaning against a lamp-post; a second showed him beside Lloyd-Jones at the sea-shore, on a Sunday school outing where he'd first been drawn into spiritual conversation; the third showed him as a smart, clean-shaven fellow whose life focused in the gospel. Under each photo was a single caption: Lost, Found, Saved.[1] Psalm 46 is something like that: there are three pictures. Of course, the keynote is in verse 1, which is the confession of faith and 'proposition' of the psalm with the sense that God is *still* our refuge

---

1   Iain H. Murray, *David Martyn Lloyd-Jones: The First Forty Years* (Edinburgh: Banner of Truth, 1982), p. 237.

and strength—in what may be (vv. 1-3), in what always is (vv. 4-7), and in what will be (vv. 8-11). Let's take a closer look at the pictures.

First picture: **God's people amid the chaos** (vv. 1-3). First off, we hear the confession of faith ('God is our refuge and strength,' v. 1a) followed by the past experience that forms the basis for that confession ('a well-proved help in troubles,' v. 1b), which in turn provides the basis for ongoing confidence ('Therefore, we are not going to fear,' v. 2a). Now we have never yet faced total chaos, but on the basis of God's help to date we do not fear even what we have not yet experienced, what is yet beyond us and unknown. The logic is the same as David pressed on King Saul: 'Yahweh who delivered me from the paw of the lion and from the paw of the bear will deliver me from the hand of this Philistine' (1 Sam. 17:37). What we need to *know* is not how bad the assault will be but only how adequate our resources are.

Note the possibility the psalmist paints in verses 2-3:

> Therefore, we are not going to fear
>> when the earth changes,
>> when the mountains topple into the heart of the seas!
>> Let its waters roar, let them foam!
>> Let the mountains tremble in its raging!

Such chaos implies serious questions and doubts about God's control. Note the use of the verb 'topple' (*mwt*) in the last of verse 2. In the passive, it is often translated 'be moved.' But it is the verb used in Psalm 93:1, where we are assured that 'Yahweh reigns' and so the world 'shall never be moved.' Psalm 96:10, same story. In Psalm 104:5, Yahweh has 'set the earth on its foundations, so that it should never be moved.' Because Yahweh is in control, the world, the earth, will not 'topple' or 'be moved.' But here in Psalm 46 there is the 'What if?' But *what if* the mountains topple into the heart of the seas? Is the psalm saying: Even when everything is so crumbly and chaotic that even God doesn't appear to be in control, *even then* God is our refuge and strength? He is depicting a worst-case scenario.

Why does the psalmist paint such an extreme picture unless to tell you that there are or will be times when God's people might feel their whole world is caving in? We can't be precise about what form this upheaval may take. It could be cosmic upheaval or geological disaster. Charles Wesley had occasion to apply the psalm in this way. On February 8, 1750, a severe earthquake shook London; actually, three distinct shakes. Residents in panic rushed into the streets. Exactly a month later a more violent one struck. At 5:15 in the morning Wesley was preaching (!), and the quake violently shook the 'Foundry' building where they met. Amid the screams, Charles immediately cried out, 'Therefore will we not fear, though the earth be moved, and the hills be carried into the midst of the sea: for the Lord of hosts is with us....'[2]

Others, however, think that the psalm may be depicting political or international disturbances under the guise of physical upheaval. Jesus has told us that such distresses would certainly characterize the present age (Mark 13:5-13).[3] There will be deception (vv. 5-6), wars

---

2   Arnold A. Dallimore, *A Heart Set Free: The Life of Charles Wesley* (Westchester, IL: Crossway, 1988), p. 173.
3   Whatever view one takes of the Olivet Discourse, Jesus' description in e.g., Mark 13:5-13, has the *present age* in view.

(v. 7), conflicts between nations and kingdoms (v. 8a), earthquakes and famines (v. 8b), persecution (vv. 9-11), betrayal (v. 12), and pervasive hatred of Jesus' people (v. 13). In short, our world is pretty much unglued.

But our psalm began by focusing on God (v. 1). What God is it, then, who is 'our refuge and strength'? In answer, let's bring in the psalm's refrain from verses 7 and 11, alongside verse 1. Clearly, He is *the God of all resources*, He is 'Yahweh of hosts,' the One who commands and has authority over all the forces of the universe; He is Lord of all legions (cf. Matt. 26:53). He is *the God of all grace*: He is 'Yahweh,' the name that commemorates the assurance in Exodus 3:12, 'But I will be with you,' and also 'the God of Jacob,' the God who pledges Himself in covenant to wobbly and undeserving people. And He is *the God of all circumstances*. He is our 'refuge' (v. 1), our protection and shelter in trouble, but also our 'high fortress' (vv. 7, 11). This latter word refers to a place up high out of the reach of danger and threat. So, we may say that sometimes Yahweh is a refuge in the midst of trouble and other times He lifts us clear up above it. In any case, verse 1b is clear: He is a well-proved help 'in troubles.' Please note the *plural*—in any and many troubles as they are. What 1 Peter 1:6 calls 'many colored trials.'

Here then are God's people amid the chaos. But in verses 1-3 it seems as if the sons of Korah had a sneak preview and were nearly singing Romans 8:35: 'Who shall separate us from the love of Christ? Shall tribulation

---

Prophecy 'experts' and sensationalist speakers may allege wars and international conflicts and earthquakes and famines are sure-fire signs of the end. They are not (cf. v. 7b)—they are the 'gunk' that takes place in the 'present age.'

or distress or persecution or famine or nakedness or peril or sword?'

Now the second picture: **God's presence in the city** (vv. 4-7). Verse 4 begins with, literally, 'A river!' Readers need to get the literary 'feel' of the psalm here. After the boiling, roiling, crashing seas of verses 2-3, there is, suddenly, this peaceful river. Sometimes you may read furrow-browed critics who claim that, to keep the symmetry of the psalm, the refrain of verses 7 and 11 should also occur after verse 3. But that is all wrong. That would screw up the abrupt contrast the psalmist wants to depict. He wants you to 'hear' the difference between the world falling apart and a place of quiet and peace. That's the way he begins the second segment of the psalm, and we should note then how these verses fit into the whole psalm. It looks like this:

Earth and chaos, vv. 1-3
    River and city, vv. 4-7
Earth and battlefield, vv. 8-11

Verses 4-7 suggest that God's people dwell in a sort of 'cosmological sandwich.' What then do we find here?

We find, as noted, a *strange peace* (v. 4). No sooner do we read, 'A river!,' than we can't help but think of Genesis 2:10, 'And a river was flowing out of Eden.' The allusion (if it is that) implies we catch a whiff of paradise in the middle of the trash and turmoil and tremors of our verses-2-and-3-world.

During the War between the States, Grant, the northern general, went out to inspect the lines of his Federal troops near Chattanooga. At one point he reached a spring that both Federal and Confederate soldiers frequented. There by the spring was a soldier in blue uniform, with his musket beside him. Grant asked him what corps he belonged to; the fellow got up, saluted, and averred that he was one of Longstreet's men! He was a Confederate yet wearing northern blue! But 'before they went their separate ways, Union commander and Confederate private had quite a chat.'[4] They were enemies. There was a war going on. But for a few moments in late 1863 there was a bit of peace in the middle of it all. And the Lord tends to do that for His people—to give them a settledness even in their topsy-turvy circumstances.

There is also the *big secret* (vv. 5-6, esp. v. 5a). Why won't, why doesn't, the city of God 'topple'? Here we have our verb *mwṭ* again; I have translated it 'topple' in all three occurrences to bring out the word/verb-play. God's city will 'not topple' (v. 5a), while mountains may topple into the seas (v. 2b) and kingdoms have toppled (v. 6). And the reason for the city's resilience is simply: 'God is in the midst of her.' That's the 'big secret.' Perhaps the situation is analogous to Mark 4:37-38: you are not likely to perish if Jesus is in the boat with you.

There's also the matter of the *right time* (v. 5b): 'God will help her when morning breaks.' The city will not topple, but if God must help her, then the city must suffer assault. But His help comes 'when morning breaks,' or, literally, 'at the turning of the morning.' This phrase conjures up Israel's escape from Pharaoh and Co. at the exodus. Note Exodus 14:27: 'So Moses stretched out his hand over the sea, and the sea returned to its

---

4 Bruce Catton, *This Hallowed Ground* (Garden City, NY: Doubleday, 1955), p. 292.

normal course at the turning of the morning. And as the Egyptians fled into it, Yahweh shook off the Egyptians into the midst of the sea.' This phrase, 'at the turning of the morning,' is only found in Exodus 14:27 and here in our psalm. One suspects the writer wanted readers to recall that exodus episode.

We should ponder this. God seems to have a pattern of morning deliverances. How many of us have pondered Psalm 30:5, 'Weeping may come stay in the evening, but at morning a shout of joy!' And there may be a specific 'morning deliverance' in the background of this psalm. This can be tricky because, aside from some definite indication, we cannot always be certain about a proposed historical setting. But some scholars think that the assault of Sennacherib, the Assyrian king (against Judah and Jerusalem in 701 B.C.), may be the life-situation our psalm reflects. He had reduced King Hezekiah of Judah to dire straits (cf. Isa. 1:7-9) and was ready to strangle Jerusalem into submission. The whole story is in 2 Kings 18-19. But a funny thing happened one night as the Assyrians were relishing their coming victory. 'On that night the Angel of Yahweh went forth and struck down 185,000 in the camp of Assyria; and when they rose early in the morning, why, they were all corpses!' (2 Kings 19:35). That was 'the turning of the morning' in 701 B.C. King Sennacherib had a hall 38 feet by 18 feet and on its walls he had depicted his conquest of Lachish. Why all the splash over Lachish? Maybe because he couldn't have a 'Jerusalem room' because there was a terror in the night for the Assyrians—and in the morning deliverance had come.

Wasn't it the same in principle in Luke 24 and John 20? Remember the despair of those two disciples: '*We* had hoped that *he* was the one to redeem Israel' (Luke 24:21, emphasis in Greek). But the 'turning of the morning' had already come, as John 20:1 tells us: 'Early on the first day of the week, while it was still dark, Mary Magdalene came to the tomb....' God helped us at the 'turning of the morning'! So often we find grace 'at just the right time' (Heb. 4:16). And why is that? Because 'God is in the midst of her.'

The final picture: **God's peace throughout the world** (vv. 8-11). This section tells us where things are heading. There are two parts to this segment: (1) an invitation to witness (vv. 8-9), and (2) a command to submit (v. 10). Verses 8-9 speak of Yahweh in the third person, while verse 10 is Yahweh speaking for Himself in the first person.

The 'works' of Yahweh (v. 8a) are the 'desolations' (v. 8b) He makes throughout the earth. Those 'desolations' are itemized in verse 9:

> [C]ausing wars to stop to the end of the earth!
> He shatters the bow;
> he snaps the spear;
> he burns the battle-wagons in the fire!

'Causing to stop' (v. 9) refers to forcible disarmament. These 'desolations' are desolations that enforce peace. The peace does not come because governments make dreary pronouncements about 'the insanity of war' or because the UN, after endless haggling, patched together a resolution deploring war. Of course, you can update the text if you like. Look at verse 9 and substitute cruise missiles, tanks, stealth bombers, suicide bombers and terrorists, if you like. But the picture is: God brings peace by force when He decimates all the matériel of war.

Now we need to look closely at verse 10. It is God's own, first-person victory pronouncement, the climax of the psalm. Who is the audience, that is, who is addressed in verse 10, and what is the tone of the statement?

Frequently, the verse seems to be taken as a calming assurance to God's people. The traditional translation, 'Be still ...' can even be read in a very soothing voice. And then the 'application' can follow: In the middle of the world's turmoil, you must 'be still,' draw apart, and commune with God. You may even see 'Be still ...' printed on the cover of a devotional booklet that displays a placid snow that had recently fallen in Vermont in late January. You imagine you are to take your favorite study Bible—and your devotional booklet—and go off for some private communion with the Lord.

But I am convinced that is not what verse 10 is about. Contextually, the most likely addressees are the nations who are in uproar (v. 6). If He were addressing Israel, the Lord would likely have used 'Yahweh' (as in 'know that I am Yahweh') but instead He uses not the covenant name but the generic Elohim, 'God,' more suitable for pagan nations. Then the usual 'Be still' is hardly a calm invitation to engage in personal devotions or communion or the like. It is a *demand* to the warring nations to 'Stop it!' (my rendering). The verb has this sense of 'stop' or 'leave off,' and the nations are being called to leave off their hostility to God and His people and to acknowledge His sovereignty and kingship.[5] Philippians 2:9-11 would be a NT parallel.

---

5   This was Calvin's view; see also the commentaries of J. A. Alexander and Allen Ross.

However, though most likely spoken to the nations, verse 10b is the basic statement about last things that you need in order to endure. Verse 10 really is equivalent to the first half of the Lord's Prayer. And here, verse 10 critiques me, for though I claim membership in 'the city of God,' my idolatry is such that I am more concerned with being comfortable in my little realm of life than that God's kingship be visible throughout the earth. 'I will be exalted among the nations, I will be exalted throughout the earth!' That statement, then, which anchors and secures me, also exposes me and calls me to dust and ashes over my selfishness and self-absorbed navel-gazing. And yet this word is my stay. I know where things are heading. I know how they will come out.

You may remember that 'Peanuts' cartoon. Lucy and Linus are looking out the window at pouring rain. 'Boy, look at it rain,' Lucy exclaims, 'What if it floods the whole world?' Linus counters that possibility: 'It will never do that. In the ninth chapter of Genesis, God promised Noah that would never happen again, and the sign of the promise is the rainbow.' Relieved, Lucy confesses that he has taken a great load off her mind, to which Linus replies: 'Sound theology has a way of doing that.'

Verse 10 is that 'sound theology.' This is the Word for you who hang on to Yahweh though you are a fragile piece of humanity seeming to be at the mercy of shaking mountains and crashing earth and the political purgatory of nations.

Psalm 47

To the music leader. Belonging to the sons of Korah. A psalm.

(1) All peoples, clap hands!
Raise a shout to God
   with a ringing sound!

(2) For Yahweh Most High is fearful
   —a great king over all the earth.

(3) He subdues peoples under us
   —and nations under our feet;

(4) he chooses our inheritance for us
   —the pride of Jacob whom he loves. Selah.

(5) God has gone up with a shout,
Yahweh at the sound of a horn.

(6) Sing praises to God,
   sing praises;
sing praises to our king,
   sing praises;

(7) for God is king of all the earth,
   sing praises with skill.

(8) God reigns over (the) nations;
God sits on his holy throne.

(9) The princes of the peoples have gathered together,
   the people of the God of Abraham;
for the shields of the earth belong to God;
   he is highly exalted.

9

Victory in the Air

By 'victory in the air' I'm not referring to a successful war-time aerial bombing mission but to the atmosphere and attitude among a people, in this case, the people of Judah in Psalm 47. The psalm has such a celebratory mood about it. Verse 1 is almost rowdy:

> All peoples, clap hands!
> Raise a shout to God
>   with a ringing sound!

Psalm 47 is a celebration of Yahweh's kingship. And royal celebrations tend to be impressive. Even somber ones. At the time of writing, we are only weeks after the funeral of Queen Elizabeth II. I don't mean to be irreverent, I know it was, after all, a funeral, but—if British readers will pardon me, I remember saying to myself, 'Those Brits really know how to put on a show!' Not a celebration, as such, but singularly impressive, at least to us non-monarchical folks. How much more should be a celebration of the kingship of the living God.

It's hard to detect how Psalm 47 is put together, and going through various options would put readers to sleep. The most convincing pattern I've found is one that takes verse 5 as the mid-point and 'hinge' of the psalm. Fleshed out, the psalm looks like this:

All peoples to praise, vv. 1-2
   God's provision for Israel, vv. 3-4
      Ascension, v. 5
   Praise from Israel, vv. 6-7
Peoples have gathered, vv. 8-9

It's a shame to treat such an ecstatic psalm with such a pedantic outline, but that is what I mean to do. It's the only way I've figured out in which to lay bare the reasoning and claims of the psalm. So let me highlight three key words or ideas that can take us into Psalm 47.

The first such term is **confirmation** (vv. 1-4). However, before getting at the 'confirmation' matter, let's soak up the surprise in the introductory command (vv. 1-2).

One surprise is that the psalm, at least at the beginning, is not addressed to Israel (or Judah). 'All peoples, clap hands! Raise a shout to God with a ringing sound!' 'All peoples' are gentiles, pagans, those outside the circle of the covenant. But they are to shout to God (v. 1), to Yahweh Most High (v. 2). The psalmist refuses to 'accept the idea that different peoples have a right to different faiths.'[1] Such a holy 'arrogance,' such an insistent

---

1   Derek Kidner, *Psalms 73–150*, TOTC (London: Inter-Varsity, 1975), p. 411 (on Psalm 117).

dogmatism about Israel's faith. So often the Bible seems to go out of its way to be offensive. 'There is a God you should enthusiastically worship and He is ours.'

Then part of the rationale for verse 1 comes in verse 2: 'For Yahweh Most High is fearful—a great king over all the earth.' There may even be an offensive 'dig' in this. Of course, we can't be certain about the historical setting of this psalm, but there are some scholars who think that Psalms 46–48 admirably fit the situation of 2 Kings 18–19 (and Isaiah 36–37), when Sennacherib, king of Assyria, was ready to crush Hezekiah and Jerusalem in 701 B.C. And, if you recall from the last chapter, the Angel of Yahweh paid a visit to the Assyrian camp and eliminated thousands of troops in their sleeping bags (2 Kings 19:35). Now if that event stands backstage of this psalm, then calling Yahweh a 'great king' may carry a special edge. That was how the kings of Assyria routinely described themselves. For example, in his annals Sennacherib identifies himself: 'Sennacherib, the great king, the mighty king, king of the universe, king of Assyria, king of the four quarters (of the earth)....'[2] Could there be an innuendo in verse 2, so much as to say, 'Nuts to that! "Great king" is lingo fit only for Yahweh!'

But now we come to the 'confirmation' idea. Verse 2 claims that Yahweh is 'fearful' and 'a great king over all the earth,' but what evidence is there for that? It seems to me that verses 3-4 supply that—Yahweh shows He is a great king by what He does for Israel:

---

2   D. D. Luckenbill, *Ancient Records of Assyria and Babylonia*, 2 vols. (London: Histories and Mysteries of Man, 1989), 2:115.

> He subdues peoples under us
>   —and nations under our feet;
> he chooses our inheritance for us
>   —the pride of Jacob ....

There is a similar pattern in Psalm 117. There the first verse calls on 'all nations' and 'all peoples' to praise Yahweh, while verse 2 supplies the reason: '*For* [emphasis mine] great is his unfailing love over *us...*' [my emphasis again]. Pagans are called to worship Yahweh *because of* the way He has dealt with Israel. The same logic seems to hold between verses 1-2 and 3-4 here in Psalm 47, or at least verses 3-4 confirm why or how Yahweh is a great king.

Now a bit of picky stuff about verbs. The ESV and NIV translate the verbs in verses 3-4 as past tenses, likely thinking of how the Lord gave victory over other peoples under Joshua (the 'conquest') and granted the land ('our inheritance') to the twelve tribes at the time. But the form of the Hebrew verbs here does not naturally refer to the past but to the future (AV, NKJV) or present (NJB, NASB). I have translated them as present tense verbs. They refer to what God does repeatedly for Israel or will finally do for them. Yahweh gives them victories (v. 3) and a place (v. 4, 'our inheritance,' the land).

The focus in verses 3-4 is on Yahweh's *provision* for His people. The 'thinking' of the psalm, then, seems to be: All peoples, shout in worship to God (v. 1), a great king (v. 2), who shows how fearful and great He is by His provision (vv. 3-4a) for His people. But there is more than provision in verses 3-4. There is also *affection*: note how the text refers to the land or inheritance as 'the pride of Jacob whom he loves' (v. 4b). I take 'Jacob' as referring to Jacob and all his people. Yahweh's love for His people should lead 'peoples' to adore Him as well.

The late German theologian, Helmut Thielicke, tells of an incident in his childhood school days. He and certain other lads took a dislike to Hans, a schoolmate with a brilliant memory but whom they thought to be somewhat phony. They decided to give Hans a thrashing. However, on the morning when the attack was to be made, something happened that stymied that plan. On that day Hans' father, very respected in town, had taken the same route that his son took to school. When they said goodbye to each other in front of the school, the 'thugs' saw how affectionately the father stroked his son's hair and patted his cheek. Then, as they parted, they both kept turning round to wave at one another. That nullified the attack. Thielicke admits that they could not have formulated their thinking at that point but the idea seemed to be that 'whoever was loved by such a father stood under a protective taboo and could not be molested.'[3] The affection displayed stirred a certain respect and awe. So it should be for 'all peoples,' the psalm argues. All peoples then should acclaim God (v. 1), for Yahweh is a great king over the whole earth (v. 2) and confirms that He is by the way He cares for Israel, giving them victories over nations (v. 3) and supplying them with His bounty (v. 4)—because He loves them. The reasoning still remains: shouldn't the nations, and especially the pagans who have sought to crush God's people, get the point? Shouldn't they see there is something uncanny

---

3   Helmut Thielicke, *Notes from a Wayfarer* (New York: Paragon House, 1995), p. 21.

about the church of Jesus that is still alive and sustained in this battered and battering world? Ought it not to prove scary to them, to stir awe and fear?

Secondly, note that verses 5-7 speak of what we may call **realization**. Verse 5 is the hinge of the psalm and depicts God as 'the mighty conqueror [who] has ascended his throne'.[4] But who then is addressed in verses 6-7? Five times they are told to 'sing praises,' or as we could render it, 'psalm it'! I think the people of Judah are addressed. That seems the more natural inference from the words 'our king' in verse 6b. What then is to drive or spur these praises they are to sing? The *realization* that God is king of all the earth (v. 7a). The logic is clear: 'Sing praises [v. 6a], *for* God is king of all the earth [v. 7a].' Not only the peoples at large (v. 1) are to praise Him as a great king (v. 2), but so are His own people who own Him as 'our king.' It's the doctrine of 7a that drives the praise of verse 6. That is, if His people fully realize the truth of verse 7a.

Sometimes that can be a problem. Think of Jeremiah. Chapter 32 of his prophecy tells how Babylonian forces are nearly ready to crush Judah and Jerusalem. Hanamel, Jeremiah's cousin, has a field in Anathoth (Jeremiah's hometown) and he wants Jeremiah to buy it. Jeremiah does so, going through all the proper legal hoops. It was a sign-action. Even when Judah is about to be smooshed, Jeremiah's purchase was a sign that 'houses and fields and vineyards will again be bought in this land' (Jer. 32:15). Jeremiah goes along with the whole affair and then he

---

4   Allen Ross, *A Commentary on the Psalms*, 3 vols. (Grand Rapids: Kregel, 2013), 2:112. 'Book Two' of the Psalms seems to prefer Elohim ('God') when referring to Israel's deity, but here in verse 5 (and v. 2) 'Yahweh', the personal, covenant name of God also appears.

prays (vv. 16-25). In his prayer, he rehearses Yahweh's great and mighty acts and says, 'Nothing is too hard for you!' (v. 17). Then, at the end of his prayer, he so much as asks, 'Why did you want me to buy that field when the Babylonians are going to gobble up the land? Isn't that rather futile?' When Yahweh responds He essentially says, 'Jeremiah, did you really mean that in your prayer—that nothing is too hard for me? (v. 27). If that's the case, then even if the land is about to be conquered and the people carted off in exile, don't you suppose I, for whom nothing is too hard, can still bring about a future in which folks are back in the land, wheeling and dealing over real estate? Is that too hard for me? Did you realize what you were saying in your prayer?'

So here in Psalm 47. If we realize and grasp the import of God as 'king of all the earth' (v. 7a), then it should ignite our praises (vv. 6, 7b). But in such a case 'God is king of all the earth' must be a lively conviction, not an ossified creed. Our theology is important, but it must really grab us if it is to infect our worship with delight.[5]

Thirdly, we can say that **incorporation** is the term that summarizes verses 8-9. Since God 'reigns over the nations' (v. 8a), He clearly has *jurisdiction* over 'the shields of the earth' (v. 9b). This latter term may refer to rulers, or, as Allen Ross prefers, to those who carried the shields, that is, the powerful warriors of the earth, all of whom belong to God 'because he has subdued them and rules over them.'[6] But there is more than His

---

5   Verse 7b tells us to sing praises 'with skill.' GW paraphrases it as 'Make your best music for him'! Worship should never be sloppy or haphazard or nonchalant. It—He—is worth our best efforts.

6   Ross, 2:115.

jurisdiction here—there is His *congregation*: 'the princes of the peoples have gathered together, the people of the God of Abraham' (v. 9a). We would normally take this last phrase as describing the covenant people Israel. But not here; the 'people of the God of Abraham' seems to refer to the 'peoples' who've gathered, peoples beyond and outside of Israel (cf. v. 1). Quite a surprise. A bit of a jaw-dropper.

And yet perhaps not such a shock. This sort of congregation is really part of God's *obligation*, for the promise He gave Abraham spoke of this privilege: 'And in you all the families of the ground shall be blessed' (Gen. 12:3). Yahweh had committed Himself to bring blessing beyond the bounds of Abraham's physical seed, to 'all the families of the ground'—and here in verse 9 is an expectation of it. It's just that it catches us by surprise when we discover it in this psalm.

Perhaps it's something like the events of December 23, 1783, when George Washington came before Congress and relinquished his commission as military commander, 'underscoring civilian control in the new republic.' In London, when George III was informed that Washington would resign and return to private life, he replied, 'If he does that, sir, he will be the greatest man in the world.'[7] Apparently, a staggering thought. A man giving up such power. Who could think of it? So here. Gentile peoples, beyond the pale of the covenant, simply described as 'the people of the God of Abraham.' It's a kind of preview of Jesus' program: 'And I have other sheep, which are

---

7 Jay Winik, *The Great Upheaval* (New York: HarperCollins, 2007), p. 51.

not of this fold; them also I must bring, and they shall hear my voice, and there will be one flock, one shepherd' (John 10:16). 'Other sheep'—Jesus brings to pass the promise of Genesis 12:3. And because of that, many of us gentiles have slithered, scurried, and sometimes hustled into the kingdom of God.

Psalm 48

A song. A psalm. Belonging to the sons of Korah.

(1) How great Yahweh is!
How much he should be praised!
In the city of our God,
the mountain of his holiness.

(2) Beautiful and high,
joy of all the earth,
Mt. Zion,
the far reaches of the north [Zaphon],
the city of the great King.

(3) God in her strongholds;
he is known as a high fortress.

(4) For, why!, the kings assembled,
they pressed on together.

(5) **They** have seen,
truly they're dumbfounded,
they are terrified,
they take to their heels.

(6) Trembling seizes them there,
anguish—like a woman giving birth.

(7) With an east wind you shatter the ships of Tarshish!

(8) As we have heard,
       so we have seen
       in the city of Yahweh of hosts,
       in the city of our God.
    God will secure her forever. Selah.

(9) We have thought, O God, on your unfailing love
       in the midst of your temple.

(10) Your praise keeps pace with your name, O God,
                to the ends of the earth;
          your right hand is full of righteousness.

(11) Let Mt. Zion be glad,
       let the daughters of Judah rejoice
          because of your judgments.

(12) Go around Zion
          and take a circuit around her;
          count her towers.

(13) Take note of her defenses;
       pass between her strongholds;
       so that you can tell (of it)
          to the next generation,

(14) that this (is) God,
          our God,
          forever and ever.
       He will guide us forever.

10

DON'T MESS WITH ZION!

I've been reading some Louis L'Amour westerns. One often meets a scene in which a local tough guy thinks he can handle a visitor to his town, one that Mr. Tough doesn't think amounts to much. It might be one of the Sackett brothers or the protagonist in another story. But the local tough guy ends up getting unexpectedly and thoroughly clobbered in a fist fight. Maybe the visitor should have told him: Don't mess with me. That seems to be the undertow of Psalm 48, a sort of warning to hostile nations, 'Don't mess with Zion.' The psalm is often called a 'song of Zion' and celebrates a decisive victory over the then bullies of the world. Praise is the dominant note, so we'll develop our treatment under that theme.

Note first, then, in verses 1-3 what we can call **Praise —and location**. The praise is ecstatic: 'How great Yahweh is! How much he should be praised!' (v. 1a).

Then the psalm goes on to speak of where this praise should be found, the place where it should be given:

> In the city of our God,
>> the mountain of his holiness.
> Beautiful and high,
> joy of all the earth,
> Mt. Zion,
>> the far reaches of Zaphon,
>> the city of the great King (vv. 1b-2).

That is quite a mailing address.

Let's touch on some of the connotations it may hold. The city is dubbed 'the mountain of his holiness,' or as some render it, 'his holy hill' (cf. NET). In some contexts holiness/holy carries the idea of being sacrosanct, secure, or under protection. In Joel 3:17, when Yahweh speaks of His restoring of His 'holy mountain,' He assures that 'Jerusalem shall be holy—and strangers will no longer pass through it,' i.e., it will be off limits to depredation; on the contrary, it will be protected and secure. Jeremiah 2:3 speaks of Israel's early days in the wilderness and says, 'Israel was holy to Yahweh, the firstfruit of his harvest—all who ate on him became guilty, disaster came on them.' Being 'holy,' again, meant they were 'off limits' and under special protection. Or one can think of Jeremiah 31:40. It speaks of the future restoration of Jerusalem and of a large extent of it that will be 'holy to Yahweh,' and then adds: 'It shall not be uprooted or overthrown any more for ever' (RSV). Therefore, off limits, protected. Given that our psalm celebrates a deliverance from external attack, the 'off limits' idea may appropriately hover over this 'mountain-of-his-holiness' language.

But this place, Mt. Zion, is also called 'the joy of all the earth.' How is that so? Perhaps this is an anticipation of Zion's future. One thinks of Isaiah 2:1-4, where 'all the nations' and 'many peoples' flow up (!) to Yahweh's mountain, are converted and seek His instruction, 'for,' verse 3b explains, 'out of Zion torah will go out and the word of Yahweh from Jerusalem.' Zion is the locale where converted pagans are going to salivate after Yahweh's Word. If that is the ultimate future of Zion (in spite of Israel/Judah's dismal infidelity in the meantime), it can indeed be billed as 'the joy of all the earth.'

Then the psalm calls Zion 'the far reaches of Zaphon,' which is probably a bit mysterious to us. 'Zaphon' is the usual word for 'north,' but here the term is probably used as a place name and not as a geographical direction. The psalmist may be making a side glance at pagan mythology. Nahum Sarna points out:

> In Ugaritic literature, Zaphon is the name of a holy mountain on which Baal, the foremost Canaanite god, had his palace, and to which the gods were summoned to assemble.[1]

The psalmist may be making a deliberate dig at paganism here, as if to say: 'So, you've heard that Zaphon is the northern mountain where the gods assemble? That's a bunch of poppycock: Zion is Zaphon! Zion is the place

---

1   Nahum M. Sarna, *On the Book of Psalms* (New York: Schocken, 1993), p. 157. The term also appears in Isaiah 14:13, where the king of Babylon tries to inflate himself toward deity; cf. John L. Mackay, *A Study Commentary on Isaiah*, 2 vols. (Darlington: Evangelical Press, 2008), 1:352.

where *Yahweh* dwells' (cf. Joel 3:17). Indeed, God is 'in her strongholds,' Himself a 'high fortress' (v. 3).

These are some of the items that help to 'color' Jerusalem or Zion in this psalm. It is God's place where God's people are, and clearly the psalm revels in this *place*. So don't go running off to John 4 and quoting verse 21 as an excuse to avoid the *place-ness* of this text. It was the dirt and gravel and rock of Zion that God defended here, 'Mount Zion, which he loves' (Ps. 78:68). And is not God's praise frequently tied to place, to location, even in our own experience? It was that way for George Whitefield. Late in life, he looked back and exclaimed,

> I know the place! It may be superstitious, perhaps, but whenever I go to Oxford I cannot help running to that place where Jesus Christ first revealed himself to me and gave me the new birth.[2]

And the Puritan, Walter Pringle, told his children the exact places where certain things happened to him. His first experience of prayer occurred 'at the northeast of Stitchel Hall,' and later he committed his new-born son to God 'at the plum tree on the north side of the garden door.'[3] God has a way of marking places in both the individual and corporate experience of His people. Here it is Zion, the place of atoning sacrifice, of stellar deliverance, and exuberant praise.

Verses 4-8 contain the second movement of the psalm; we can call this section **Praise—and devastation**. The

2   Arnold A. Dallimore, *George Whitefield*, 2 vols. (Westchester, IL: Cornerstone, 1981), 1:77.
3   Leland Ryken, *Worldly Saints* (Grand Rapids: Zondervan, 1986), p. 209.

general scene is one of kings forming a coalition to assault Zion, but God decimates, terrifies, and destroys them.

We're used to hearing in the Psalms of kings and nations rebelling against Yahweh and moving to destroy His people (see, e.g., Psalms 2, 74, 79, 83, 124, 129). The keynote in Psalm 48 is how quickly and decisively the attackers are neutralized. Even verse 4b may stress this; it can be translated, as Alexander prefers, 'they passed away together.' As if saying, no sooner do they assemble than they exit the scene. I have translated the verse as 'they pressed on together,' i.e., continuing and following up their attack. It's hard to decide; one can justify either translation. In any case, these hostile kings are confused, terrified, and disposed of (vv. 5-6). There's a word picture in verse 7. 'Ships of Tarshish' are probably the large, cargo-carrying ships, the 'heavy hitters' of the sea.[4] But God smashes them up and sends them to Davy Jones' locker. 'The ships of Tarshish' may be a figure for the hefty, attacking kings. God's people have heard that He defends His people like this—and now they have actually seen it in Jerusalem (v. 8). It's an assurance for the future (v. 8c).

Some contemporary readers may be bothered by this combination of praise and devastation. It seems so terribly brutal (because it is). One can almost imagine someone asking if those opposing kings couldn't have received some counseling first. Well, they did—see Psalm 2:10-12! The plain fact is that verses 4-7 contain nasty stuff, but there's no avoiding it: if there is to be deliverance for God's people there must be destruction for their enemies. Remember

---

4   Cf NBD, 3rd ed., 1153.

the exodus: 'So Yahweh saved Israel on that day from the hand of the Egyptians; *and Israel saw the Egyptians dead on the seashore*' (Exod. 14:30, emphasis mine).

Examples of this principle are legion. One easily thinks of July 1588 when Philip II's Spanish Armada came to unseat England's Elizabeth and to restore Catholicism in the land. They came with 130 ships, over 8,000 sailors, taking along 19,000 soldiers. There were 30,000 troops with the Duke of Parma in Flanders, whose assistance the Spanish hoped to secure in the process for a march on London. The English had eighty-two ships and at one point had only enough ammunition for one day's fighting. July 29 was the main action. English shot penetrated Spanish wooden hulls, even though three feet thick. Blood flowed from Spanish decks into the sea. At the day's close, the Armada had lost 4,000 men, 4,000 more were wounded, and the next day's winds carried the broken, surviving ships into the North Sea. The Armada had already run into a damaging storm on the way but nevertheless had pressed on—to meet this disaster. Now injured ships and starving men tried to negotiate the sea north of Scotland and to come down west of Ireland on their way back to Spain, but day after day a ship would sink, and dead men were heaved into the waters; at Sligo, Ireland, over 1,000 drowned Spaniards washed up on the beach. Fifty-four of the 130 ships returned, and 10,000 men, most wounded or sick. Terrible devastation, but, for England, welcome salvation.[5] Elizabeth's commemorative medal

---

5   See Will and Ariel Durant, *The Age of Reason Begins*, *The Story of Civilization: Part VII* (New York: Simon and Schuster, 1961), pp. 33-38.

bore the legend: 'God blew with His winds and they were scattered.'[6]

Britain's 'salvation' required Spain's destruction. That is the way it has to be. I'm inclined to think Psalm 48 has in view the recent deliverance from Assyria's threat on Jerusalem in 701 B.C. (as noted in expositions of Psalms 46 and 47). If so, then when folks in Judah went out that morning and saw myriads of Assyrian troops stone dead in their camp (2 Kings 19:35), surely they did not say, 'Oh, how I hate violence and killing! Why can't these conflicts be settled by peaceful means?' No, you are meant to look on those corpses and sing, 'He comes to break oppression, to set the captive free.'[7] In this sad, vicious, Yahweh-hating world deliverance often involves destruction—else there is no deliverance. The Shorter Catechism asks 'how Christ executes the office of a king?' and answers: 'Christ executes the office of a king, in subduing us to himself, in ruling and defending us, and in restraining and conquering all his and our enemies' (Q/A 26). Not all that defending, restraining, and conquering can be calm, peaceful, and bloodless. But we praise Him for it.

Finally, we come to the third section of the psalm, verses 9-14, where the emphasis is on **Praise—and reflection**. The psalmist hits the 'reflection' note right away: 'we have thought, O God, on your unfailing love' (v. 9), an unfailing love shown in His delivering them from the assaults of verses 4-8, deliverance that was an

---

6   S. M. Houghton, *Sketches from Church History* (Edinburgh: Banner of Truth, 1980), p. 150.

7   From James Montgomery's hymn, 'Hail to the Lord's Anointed.'

evidence of His 'righteousness' (v. 10) and was one of His 'judgments' (v. 11). And now the people (the verbs are imperative plurals) are urged to take a local tour and ponder the evidence:

> Go around Zion
>> and take a circuit around her;
>> count her towers.
> Take note of her defenses;
>> pass between her strongholds (vv. 12-13a).

They are to see that none of the towers has been toppled, everything is in place as before, nothing has been mashed down or destroyed. Which means they have a testimony to pass on to the following generation (v. 13b). I think the testimony follows in verse 14. I don't translate the opening particle as 'For,' but as 'that' (as ESV, NJB)— expressing the content of their testimony:

> that this (is) God,
>> our God,
>> forever and ever.
> **He** will guide us forever (v. 14).[8]

Maria Linke, who was later a prisoner of the Russians and suffered their brutality, tells of a frightening day in Berlin in April 1945. She was a civilian interpreter in a factory among Russian workers who evidently had come to Germany near the beginning of World War II. Berlin was subject to incessant bombing. Near dusk on

---

8 The last line of verse 14 is difficult. Some translate 'he will guide us unto (or, beyond) death' (cf. NIV's paraphrase, 'even to the end'). However, the two forms at the end of the verse can be read as one word (and with different vowels) and be taken as 'forever' (so LXX, NRSV; cf. NEB, 'eternally'). I have opted for the latter.

this particular day, Maria was hurrying on foot to find her father at their home near the center of Berlin. Her mother, sister, and others had been evacuated but her father remained. She needed to get to him to tell him that as soon as the factory terminated their work, she would come home to stay with him and care for him. She had no assurance, of course, that her father was still alive. She hadn't been home in a long time. There was no transportation. The tracks of the train she would have taken were twisted, a couple of cars lying on their sides. Rubble everywhere. She ran and stumbled, then found she was wading water. A worker explained: water main broken. She sloshed on, shivering from the icy wind. She ran and fell and ran on. Hardly any recognizable landmarks. She asked someone, 'Is this Bluecherstrasse?' Apparently, but all seemed wreck and ruin. The huge church on the corner, the Hertie Department Store—all gone. Concrete blocks and big timbers strewn across the street. She remembered her father's word: 'This house will be preserved.' It was a home that had sheltered a hunted Jew, had been a center of Christian witness. But her father's words seemed to mock her amid the wreckage. And then she saw it, she said, 'standing battered and alone, the only remaining building on the block!' Both he and she were overcome—he heard her factory had been bombed, yet she had come and he was there, now holding her. 'This house will be preserved.'[9]

Perhaps that anecdote can serve as an analogy or parable of Psalm 48. Especially so if the psalm has in view

---

9   Ruth Hunt, *East Wind: The Story of Maria Zeitner Linke* (Grand Rapids: Zondervan, 1976), pp. 11-13.

Yahweh's deliverance from Sennacherib and his Assyrians in 701 B.C. In his annals, Sennacherib boasts of taking forty-six of Hezekiah's walled cities, carting off 200,000 people and a horde of livestock as he ravaged much of Judah. 'Himself,' he says of Hezekiah, 'like a caged bird, I shut up in Jerusalem.'[10] Yet on that morning... there are the Assyrians dead in their camp and there is Jerusalem—with every tower untouched. 'This house will be preserved.' And when you think on that you can say with assurance, 'This is God—He will guide us forever.'

---

10 D. D. Luckenbill, *Ancient Records of Assyria and Babylonia*, 2 vols. (London: Histories & Mysteries of Man, 1989), 2:119-21.

Psalm 49

To the music leader. For the sons of Korah. A psalm.

(1) Hear this, all peoples!
    Listen, all residents of the world!

(2) Both low and high,
    rich and poor together!

(3) My mouth will speak wisdom,
    and the meditation of my heart [will speak] understanding.

(4) I will bend down my ear to a proverb;
    I will open up my riddle with a lyre.

(5) Why should I fear in days of evil,
    (when) iniquity circles round my heels?

(6) [There are] those who are trusting in their wealth,
    and they boast in their massive riches.

(7) There's no way a man can redeem another
    —he can't give to God his ransom price

(8) (Now the ransom for their life is costly,
    and he backs off forever)

(9) that he could live forever
    —never see the pit.

(10) For he sees [that] wise men die,
     both the stupid and thick-headed perish
         —and they leave their wealth to others.

(11) Their inner thought [is that] their houses are forever,
their dwellings [go on] generation after generation;
they claim lands with their names.

(12) But man will not spend the night in his pomp;
he is like the beasts that perish.

(13) This is their course—their stupidity;
but after them [men] will delight in what they say. Selah.

(14) Like sheep they are appointed to Sheol;
death will be their shepherd;
and the upright will rule over them come morning;
and their form, when Sheol consumes it, has no dwelling.

(15) But **God** will redeem my life from the power of Sheol,
for he will take me. Selah.

(16) Don't fear when a man becomes rich,
when he increases the glory of his home;

(17) for he cannot take it all when he dies,
his glory will not go down after him,

(18) for he may bless his soul while he lives
—and they praise you when you do well for yourself;

(19) he goes to the generation of his fathers;
they will never see light.

(20) Man in his pomp—and without understanding
—is like the beasts that perish.

11

WISDOM FOR THE DYING

Sometimes life scarcely gets off the ground. That morning in 1483 when Hans Luder (= Luther) brought his new-born son, Martin, for baptism, the infant mortality rate was 60 percent or more.[1] Oliver Cromwell (who is blessed or blasted according to one's disposition) was one of ten children and the only one to survive infancy.[2] That was in the 1600s, when only half of infants made it past their first year, middle age was one's thirties, and few made it beyond forty.[3] Or one can go back pre-Luther, when the 'Black Death' swept through Europe from

---

1   James M. Kittelson, *Luther the Reformer* (Minneapolis: Augsburg, 1986), p. 32.
2   Will and Ariel Durant, *The Age of Reason Begins, The Story of Civilization: Part VII* (New York: Simon and Schuster, 1961), p. 207.
3   Jay Winik, *The Great Upheaval* (New York: HarperCollins, 2007), p. 2.

1347–1400. 'A third of Europe's population perished – in some countries, half the population.'[4] But there have been advances in drugs and medical care and now, at least in more developed countries, we tend to presume that additional chronology will grace our lives. But life is always fragile and, as Psalm 49 reminds us, only the knuckle-headed and hard-hearted refuse to consider that. Here then is some wisdom for the dying.[5]

You will notice a twice-occurring refrain (vv. 12, 20) that sort of divides the psalm. However, verses 1-4 seem to be something of a prologue and can be considered under the rubric of **wisdom among the masses**.

The psalm hits us with a bit of a surprise right at the start: it's not just for Israel, for covenant people, but for covenant people and pagan people—'all peoples... all residents of the world' (v. 1). The scope is human, not just Israelite, and takes in literally everyone, both the upper-crust and those at the bottom of the economic ladder (v. 2). His claim is bold: he will speak wisdom and understanding (v. 3); if that is the case, it would be folly not to pay attention. But then in verse 4, he speaks of the *source* and *manner* of this wisdom. When he says, 'I will bend down my ear to a proverb,' he seems to be speaking of receiving divine revelation. It is something he has received rather than something he has concocted, and

---

4   N. R. Needham, *2000 Years of Christ's Power,* 5 vols. (Ross-shire: Christian Focus Publications, 2000), 2:354.

5   I always find the Psalms a struggle to understand, but ones like Psalm 49 all the more so. The meaning and sense of a number of lines can be disputed. If I stopped to discuss each one, we'd never get through the psalm. You can track what decisions I've made by consulting my translation that precedes the exposition.

he is going to present it lyrically, singing it with a lyre. He's going to deal with matters of life and death and his opening sentences say to everybody: you desperately need to pay attention to this.

Sometimes a preliminary alert like this can prove most beneficial, unless one ignores it. Bruce Catton has noted some of the problems the South should have noted before the American War between the States erupted. The South didn't have a proper transportation system. They had a bunch of mostly local railroads but the tracks were of various gauges. So, if a trainload of supplies came into a town, it would have to be unloaded, transported to the next train across town, reloaded on train cars that fit that track gauge, and move on. Then, nearly all the South's locomotives, rails, spikes, car wheels and bodies and more, came from the North. Even freight moving in wagons on country roads moved in wagons manufactured in the North. Catton sums up: 'These problems, indeed, were so grave and pointed so surely toward final defeat that one is forced to wonder how the founding fathers of the confederacy could possibly have overlooked them.'[6] Had attention been paid, perhaps a 'solution' other than a horrendous war would have been sought. That seems to be the function of verses 1-4, as if the psalmist says, 'You dare not ignore this.'

Our second segment runs from verses 5-13, which we can call **fearlessness among the powerful**. And the psalmist suggests, 'Let me begin with my problem' (vv. 5-6). He stirs up his faith in verse 5:

---

6   Bruce Catton, *The Coming Fury* (Garden City, NY: Doubleday, 1961), pp. 434-35.

Why should I fear in days of evil,
(when) iniquity circles round my heels?

But verse 6 seems to suggest why he *might* fear: 'There
are those who are trusting in their wealth.' These are
the wealthy and therefore powerful hombres who
evidently pressure, oppress, hound, and make trouble
for the psalmist and others. He seems to say, I've no
grounds to fear their threats and intimidation because
their problem (vv. 7-13) is far worse than *my* problem. His
main contention is that he can be fearless because these
'heavy hitters' are really so powerless since they enjoy
such brief tenure.

He begins by saying that the way of the wealthy and
powerful is so *futile* (vv. 7-9). All the 'massive riches'
(v. 6b) one may have are insufficient to pay God a 'ransom
price' for either ransoming another or oneself from the
clutches of 'the pit' (v. 9b). The price is too high—even
the filthy rich can't pay it (cf. v. 8).

But beyond this futility, there is something sadly
irrational about their course (vv. 10-11). The wealthy
wicked sees that all die—wise men and 'the stupid and
thick-headed' as well—and that the latter at least simply
leave all their goodies to others. He sees that but, in the
teeth of the evidence, seems to think that he can somehow
beat the ravages of death. Such folks think:[7]

their houses are forever,
their dwellings [go on] generation after generation;
they claim lands with their names (v. 11).

---

7   The first of verse 11 is a bit perplexing but the standard Hebrew
text does make sense, so I have retained it. ESV follows a slight
emendation with 'Their graves are their homes forever.'

This may imply that he expects to perpetuate his memory through his household, maybe having lands named after him. But it won't work. The building may have 'Jackson Memorial City Hall' above the entrance, but people go in and out of there and don't give a rip about who 'Jackson' was. No, verse 12 assures us, 'Man will not spend the night in his pomp.' I've translated the verb quite woodenly to point up the contrast: One not only can't perpetuate himself (v. 11), his swaggering pride can't even enjoy a one-night stay (v. 12). He dies just like old Bossy the cow (v. 12b). He should at least have taken the evidence (v. 10) to heart.

Verse 13 provides an additional sad note. It's bad enough that the rich, wicked man's course is stupid, but it's worse in that he seems to have begotten disciples: 'but after them [men] will delight in what they say' (v. 13b). There is an after-life, a *continuity* of this world-view. Others are somehow impressed with the rich man's swagger and 'philosophy,' eat up his point of view, and live accordingly. Stupidity lives on.

So our psalmist need not fear the powerful since he realizes how transitory they are, something they tend to ignore. It's a mercy when they are reminded of it. St. Nilus was a monk in the tenth century (around A.D. 940 and following) who didn't mind confronting 'important' people. He once rebuked Pope Gregory V and Emperor Otho III for the way they treated an archbishop. Later, the emperor offered Nilus any favor he might ask and Nilus retorted, 'I ask nothing from you but that you would save your soul; for you must die like every other man, and render an account to God for all your good and evil deeds.'[8] The psalmist's

---

8   Philip Schaff, *History of the Christian Church*, 8 vols. (reprint ed., Grand Rapids: Eerdmans, 1980), 4:365.

depiction should keep *any* of us from saying, 'Soul, you have many goods laid up for many years' (Luke 12:19). That's the most asinine attitude one can imagine.

I have isolated verses 14-20 as a third section that highlights **assurance among the perishing.**

A look at verse 14 shows that our writer still has man 'in his pomp' (cf. v. 12) in view. His preoccupation with this ilk brings to mind an exchange in a 'Peanuts' comic between Lucy and Schroeder. Beethoven, of course, is Schroeder's idol, and Lucy baits Schroeder with her own dogma: 'Beethoven wasn't so great!' Schroeder immediately demands an explanation for such an absurd opinion. So Lucy unloads with: 'He never got his picture on bubble gum cards, did he? Have you ever seen his picture on bubble gum cards, huh? How can you say someone is great who's never had his picture on bubble gum cards?' But our psalmist might say, if we can stoop to being anachronistic, 'But I have been describing people who *have* gotten their pictures on bubble gum cards—ones who are wealthy, powerful, influential, who have been determined to make their mark in this world.' And here, he says, is the end of those bubble-gum-card people (v. 14). 'Like sheep they are appointed to Sheol,' the realm of the dead. 'Death will be their shepherd,' not a consoling note (contrast with Ps. 23:1). 'Death' is probably personified (not deified) here and so could properly be capitalized. And, he claims, 'The upright will rule over them come morning.' 'Morning' likely indicates a new future beyond the present duress (cf. 90:14) when the tables are completely turned.[9]

---

9   The last line of verse 14 is tough. I have translated, 'And their form, when Sheol consumes it, has no dwelling.' But it is very difficult. NJPS,

In verses 16-19 the psalmist counsels his fellow believer not to fear these powerful, rich, weight-throwing folks (v. 16) since their power and 'glory' will not stay with them (v. 17). They may be pleased with themselves while they live and collect kudos and acclaim from drooling admirers (v. 18), but it all evaporates in Sheol (vv. 17, 19). Hence the refrain of verse 12 again falls like a thud (v. 20).

But I have said that this section deals with 'assurance among the perishing.' And it does. The writer spends most of his space on the perishing but the assurance is here in all its virility in verse 15: 'But *God* [emphatic] will redeem my life from the power of Sheol, for he will take me.' This hope stands in stark contrast to the doom of the oppressors in verse 14, who are 'appointed to Sheol.' There is no doubt about why he has this hope—it is God's doing; 'Elohim' is the emphatic subject—'But *God* will redeem my life....' He makes all the difference.

Furthermore, we must not miss the *personal* nature of this assurance: 'God will redeem *my* life ... for he will take *me*' (emphasis mine). It is not a corporate matter here (a 'we' statement); it is clearly individual and personal. That is so necessary in matters of assurance. Bishop Butler (d. 1752) made his mark with his *Analogy of Natural and Revealed Religion*. His faith, however, seemed to be more

---

noting the uncertain text, offers: 'And their form shall waste away in Sheol till its nobility be gone'; cf. also NET: 'Sheol will consume their bodies, and they will no longer live in impressive houses.' In spite of difficulties, J. A. Alexander holds that 'the general idea of the verse is plain, to wit, that they are now an object of envy or congratulation are soon to be deprived by death of all their coveted and boasted advantages' (*The Psalms, Translated and Explained* [reprint ed., Grand Rapids: Zondervan, 1955; first published, New York: Scribner, 1853], p. 221.

intellectual than experiential. So when he lay dying, he was in considerable distress and told his chaplain that in spite of his effort to live a good life, he was afraid to die. His chaplain replied, 'My lord, you have forgotten that Jesus Christ is a Saviour.' 'True,' said the bishop, 'but how shall I know that He is a Saviour for me?' The chaplain countered, 'My lord, it is written, Him that cometh to me I will in no wise cast out.' Here the bishop confessed, 'I am surprised that, though I have read that Scripture a thousand times over, I never felt its virtue till this moment, and now I die happy.'[10]

Then, this is a *simple* assurance. Note the words, 'for he will take me.' The verb is rather common, *laqa h,* and can be translated 'receive,' as some do. But I have kept the mundane 'take.' It has bonnie associations when connected with the end of believers' lives. We are accustomed to seeing it in Genesis 5:24: 'And Enoch walked with God, and he was not [there], for God took him.' Took him where? To Himself, I suppose. Enoch stands in stark contrast to every other hombre in Genesis 5, all of whose life paragraphs end with 'and he died.' But Enoch didn't. Why not? Because God 'took' him. Then remember the tight tension in 2 Kings 2, when everybody seems edgy and knows that Elijah is going to be 'taken' (vv. 3, 5, 9, 10) and goes up in a storm wind heavenward (v. 11). He does not die; he is 'taken.' Mysterious? Yes, but that's the text. Then in Psalm 73, after the psalmist's agonizing ordeal, we come to the assurance section and in verse 24 run into our verb again: 'You will guide me with your counsel,

---

10   Cited in Arnold A. Dallimore, *George Whitefield*, 2 vols. (Westchester, IL: Cornerstone, 1970), 1:262.

and afterwards you will take me to glory.' And then here in Psalm 49: 'for he will take me.' No details, except it involves freedom from the power of Sheol. But isn't it enough? Don't other Scriptures add more details to the believer's hope post-death? Yes, but this is pretty adequate. Isn't it very like what Jesus says in John 14:3? 'and if I go and prepare a place for you, I will come again and take you to myself, that where I am you may be also.' That gives a few more sidelights but it's still much the same: 'take you to myself.' Pretty simple, huh? And entirely adequate.

Then there is a hint that this is a *costly* assurance: 'God will *redeem* my life from the power of Sheol' (emphasis mine). The psalmist has already used this verb. He's told us that 'There's no way a man can redeem another,' to give God a ransom price, 'that he could live forever' (vv. 7, 9). But verse 15 implies that God, somehow, can pay that price. It's all unspecified here; the psalmist doesn't explain *how*. But we ourselves can't help but see the shadow of Golgotha falling across the page, can we?

Psalm 50

A psalm of Asaph.

(1) The Mighty One, God, Yahweh!
He has spoken and summoned the earth
from the rising of the sun to its setting.

(2) Out of Zion, the perfection of beauty,
God shines forth.

(3) Let our God come, and not keep silent!
Fire consumes before him,
and around him a raging storm.

(4) He calls to the heavens above
and to the earth, to judge his people.

(5) 'Gather to me my covenant ones,
those who cut a covenant with me by sacrifice.'

(6) And the heavens declare his righteousness,
yes, God himself is judging. Selah.

(7) 'Listen, my people, and I will speak;
(listen), Israel, and I will testify against you;
I am God, your God.

(8) I won't rebuke you about your sacrifices,
and your burnt offerings are continually before me.

(9) I will not take a bull from your house,
nor goats from your folds;

(10) for every animal in the forest is mine,
      the livestock on a thousand hills.

(11) I know every bird in the mountains,
      and the creatures in the field are mine.

(12) If I were hungry, I wouldn't tell you
      —for the world is mine and everything in it.

(13) Do I eat the flesh of bulls,
      and drink the blood of goats?

(14) Sacrifice a thank-offering to God
      and pay your vows to the Most High,

(15) and call on me in the day of trouble
      —I will pull you out, and you shall glorify me.'

(16) But to the wicked God says:
      'What are you doing rehearsing my statutes,
      and taking up my covenant in your mouth?

(17) But **you** have hated instruction
        and threw my words behind you.

(18) If you see a thief, you run with him,
      and you take your place with adulterers.

(19) Your mouth you have given to evil,
      and your tongue shapes deceit.

(20) You sit (and) speak against your brother,
      you bring a charge against your mother's son.

(21) These things you have done,
         and I kept quiet;
      you thought I was just like yourself.
      I will rebuke you
         and I will set (the charge) right in front of you.

(22) Get the point, you forgetters of God,
      lest I tear you apart
         and there's no one to deliver.'

(23) The one offering a thank-offering glorifies me,
      and (for) the one who sets his way (rightly),
         I will show the salvation of God.

12

JUDGMENT BEGINS AT THE HOUSEHOLD OF GOD

In my first year or so at Trinity Evangelical Divinity School I came out of a chapel service one morning next to my friend, Ron, who exclaimed, 'That was a great message—everything he said applied to somebody I know.' He was joking, of course. But it's not hard to slop into an attitude like that—that God judges 'those other folks'; surely God wouldn't scourge or criticize His own people, folks who recite the Apostles' Creed, sing 'My Jesus, I Love Thee' or 'In Christ Alone,' and take notes on the sermon? But Psalm 50 reminds us that God does indeed judge His own people, in fact, that judgment begins at the household of God (cf. 1 Peter 4:17).

Scholars sometimes see in or behind Psalm 50 a cultic ceremony, perhaps an occasion of covenant renewal. That may well be, but things get 'iffy' when trying to work out the details. The note in NET is accurate: 'This psalm takes the form of a covenant lawsuit in which the Lord comes to confront his people in a formal manner.' All very well. But how does He come? Does such confrontation happen regularly, occasionally—or how often? Perhaps Allen Ross has it right:

> It is not a description of an actual coming, and not a prophecy of a coming of the LORD to judge his people. It is a vision of a hypothetical court case—what if the LORD came today and set up court in the sanctuary to examine the worship of his people?[1]

And so, first, Asaph shows us **the God who comes** (vv. 1-6). He comes in *splendor*, immediately expressed in His triple name (v. 1a), 'The Mighty One, God, Yahweh!', literally, 'El, Elohim, Yahweh,' which can also be translated as a superlative, 'Yahweh is the greatest God.'[2] He reveals Himself from 'Zion' (v. 2) and yet the scope of His authority takes in 'the earth' (v. 1b) and He comes with Sinai-style fire before Him, raging storm about Him (v. 3b; cf. Exod. 19:16-20), which once scared the daylights out of Israel (Exod. 20:18-19). Yahweh's coming is never boring (cf. Micah 1:2-4; Nahum 1:3-6).

Perhaps this coming, however, packs a *surprise* (vv. 4-5), for God calls heaven and earth as His witnesses, and His purpose is to 'judge his people.' Pagans or heathen

---

1   *A Commentary on the Psalms*, 3 vols. (Grand Rapids: Kregel, 2013), 2:158. I think Ross means the presentation in the psalm is 'hypothetical' rather than reflecting a particular historical moment. There is nothing hypothetical about the fact that the Lord judges His people.

2   Richard S. Hess, *Joshua*, TOTC (Downers Grove, IL: Inter-Varsity, 1996), p. 292 (on Josh. 22:22).

nations are not in the dock but His own professing people, those who 'cut a covenant' with Him 'by sacrifice.' This may allude to the covenant ceremony in Exodus 24:1-8. During the Gorbachev–Reagan summit in Washington in December 1987, Mrs. Raisa Gorbachev went shopping in New York with an American Express Gold Card. That was illegal in Russia, punishable with a long prison term.[3] But she was Raisa Gorbachev: she was above the law; she was special; she was exempt. But the point of verses 4-5 is that Israelites do not get an exemption card. Will the nations be judged? Yes. But so will the covenant people.

Then, in verse 6, Asaph highlights the *standard* of God's judgment: 'the heavens declare his righteousness.' God's scrutiny and assessment will be in line with what is right and true. Sometimes that can be something of a comfort or encouragement (see 1 Cor. 4:3-4 in context). More often, it should be cause for shuddering and fear, as when the apostle proclaimed that God 'will judge the world *in righteousness* by a man whom he has appointed' (Acts 17:31, RSV; emphasis mine). It should sober God's professing people as well.

Some contemporary believers may suppose that this 'judging' the psalm speaks of is something that belongs only to the Old Testament period; surely it is not something operative in the 'new age' of fulfillment. But that flies in the face of New Testament testimony. When Paul dealt with Christians who held opposing convictions about what they could eat or what occasions they would celebrate, he cautions them with: 'But *you*—why do you

---

3   Paul Johnson, *Modern Times*, rev. ed. (New York: HarperCollins, 1991), p. 766.

judge your brother? Or also *you*—why do you despise your brother? For we *all* shall stand before the judgment seat of God' (emphasis in the Greek). He supports his point from Old Testament Scripture and then concludes, 'So then each one of us shall give account of himself to God' (Rom. 14:10, 12). Clearly, he is speaking to Christians ('each one of us'). In 2 Corinthians 5:9, Paul mentions how he and others make it their aim to please Christ, and then in verse 10 gives the rationale for that ambition: 'For we must all be seen for what we are before the judgment seat of Christ, in order that each one might receive for things done in the body, whether good or worthless.' Again, this is clearly a 'Christian' affair.

So we cannot 'duck' this. But some may see an implicit contradiction with the truth of justification. When we are 'justified by faith' (cf. Rom. 5:1) we are declared acquitted, for Jesus' sake, from all condemnation. But this 'judgment' does not counter a believer's justified status. The judgment of 2 Corinthians 5:10, for example, does not determine destiny but assesses discipleship.[4]

We have to ask ourselves how we are to respond to this God who comes to 'judge his people' (v. 4). I doubt we can do better than to take up the attitude of Tom Haire. In the 1950s, Tom Haire, a plumber and lay preacher from Ireland, apparently struck up a friendship with A. W. Tozer, a Christian and Missionary Alliance pastor then ministering in Chicago. Haire spent some time among Tozer's congregation. Right before he was scheduled to return to his homeland, Haire stopped by

---

4   See the comments of Murray J. Harris, '2 Corinthians,' EBC, 12 vols. (Grand Rapids: Zondervan, 1976), 10:349.

Chicago again to say goodbye to Tozer. Tozer expressed his surmise about Haire: 'Well, Tom, I guess you'll be going back to Ireland to preach.' 'No,' Tom retorted [imagine a thick Irish brogue], 'I intend to cancel all appointments for the next six months and spend that time preparing for the judgment seat of Christ while I can still do something about it.'[5] You can do a lot worse than that.

Secondly, in the mid-section of the psalm (vv. 7-15) we hear **the God who corrects.** Here, He will 'testify against' them (v. 7), and He begins with an it's not about this note (v. 8). I'm not confronting you because your quota of sacrifices is too low; oh no, there are plenty of them. Rather, He says: *you must realize your perversions* (vv. 8-13). We may be very rigorous about the rituals of worship and yet by our attitudes and mindset can pervert that worship. Therefore, His people must correct and re-adjust their thinking about Him—they must realize that He is not *deficient* (vv. 9-11) and therefore that He is not *dependent* (vv. 12-13).

God avows that He doesn't need sacrificial victims, doesn't have to have their bulls or goats as if His stock is depleted (v. 9), 'for,' He asserts, 'every animal in the forest is mine, the livestock on a thousand hills' (v. 10). If that is the case, then clearly He is not dependent on them and their sacrifices. In verse 12 it is as if He says: Imagine if I were hungry ..., well, I wouldn't inform you of the fact 'for the world is mine and everything in it.' Then He follows up with the argument from

---

5   James L. Snyder, *The Life of A. W. Tozer* (Ventura, CA: Regal, 2009), pp. 147-48.

absurdity: 'Do I eat the flesh of bulls and drink the blood of goats?' (v. 13).

But the argument from absurdity is not so absurd. For when an Israelite begins to think that Yahweh has *need* of sacrifices, he has begun thinking like a pagan, for nothing was more axiomatic to the pagan than that the gods and goddesses had the same needs as men and women (only on maybe a more celestial scale) and that the 'calling' of pagan worshipers was to sustain their gods. The presence of a god would be in the image of the deity. Well, maybe. First there had to be an 'opening of the mouth' ceremony for the deity to be operating in the image. Think of those times when you receive a new credit card and you have to call a particular number to 'activate' your card. Then, the deity in the image gets perhaps two meals a day. Water for washing first, then cuts of meat, and finally fruit. Music is playing throughout the repast, curtains drawn around the image, and afterwards water again for the clean-up. Of course, the food is still there; apparently, the thought was that the image consumed the food by looking at it (perhaps he or she 'inhaled').[6] But whenever we (or in this case Israel) begin to think that Yahweh needs our worship or sacrifices or devotion, we have begun operating on pagan principles and have forgotten that we worship the God of Isaiah 66:1-2a.

Jesus, you might remember, warned His disciples of this pagan 'slippage' in the matter of prayer. 'When you pray, don't babble on like the pagans do, for they think they will be heard for their much speaking' (Matt. 6:7). Pagans

---

6   See E. M. Curtis, 'Idol, Idolatry,' ABD, 3:377-78, and A. Leo Oppenheim, *Ancient Mesopotamia*, rev. ed. (Chicago: U. of Chicago Press, 1977), pp. 191-92.

pray pagan prayers because they operate on pagan *thinking*. In Psalm 50, Yahweh seeks to correct Israel's thinking. If contemporary believers think they are above such false views of God, they would do well to read the first half of J. B. Phillips' 1963 book, *Your God Is Too Small*. Ponder the 'resident policeman,' the 'parental hangover,' the 'grand old man,' 'managing director,' 'perennial grievance' and other conceptions we may subtly adopt. You may not have the same perversion as Israel in Psalm 50, but you may have one of your own—and you may find the God of Psalm 50 confronting and correcting you.

However, there's a positive aspect to God's correction here. He tells His erring people: *you must exercise your privileges* (vv. 14-15). If there is *perverted* worship (vv. 7-13), there is also *proper* worship.

Let's take a moment with verse 14a, which I've translated, 'Sacrifice a thank-offering to God.' Some, like NKJV, render it, 'Offer to God thanksgiving.' That is all right, as long as we don't take the thanksgiving to be offered apart from or instead of the sacrifice. The Lord isn't negating the sacrificial system for His Old Testament worshipers. Perhaps J. A. Alexander has caught the idea best: 'Sacrifice to God thanksgiving.' It's not that Israel is not to sacrifice, nor that thanksgiving is to be a *substitute* for their sacrifice but that their sacrifice is to be an *expression* of thanksgiving.[7] Make sure thanksgiving accompanies your sacrifice.

Back to all of verses 14-15. What is the teaching? In verse 14, God says Israel's worship should be both *thankful* (14a) and *faithful* (14b—fulfill any promises/vows you

---

7   J. A. Alexander, *The Psalms, Translated and Explained* (reprint ed., Grand Rapids: Zondervan, n.d.), p. 227.

have made). 'And …,' the first word of verse 15. Sometimes 'and' is such an important word! Here it indicates
there is more: His people should enjoy the privilege they
have in worship, namely, 'And call on me in the day of
trouble—I will pull you out, and you shall glorify me'
(v. 15).[8] How well the Lord knows His people and their
situations—how often they are in trouble; and He promises
to deliver them—*and* (the big word again) they then get
to worship with thanksgiving ('and you shall glorify
me'). That last element is easy to forget. I've always been
impressed with the clip of text in Deuteronomy 8:7-10,
where Moses tells Israel that Yahweh is bringing them
into such a good land, with water, loading them with
everything from wheat to pomegranates, from honey to
bread and so on—and then in verse 10: 'and you shall
eat and be satisfied, and [!] you shall bless Yahweh your
God for the good land that he has given you.' It seems so
natural—but it isn't. 'And you shall bless ….' How easy
it is to 'drop the ball' there. Here in verse 15, we have
emergency, deliverance, and thanksgiving, these three,
but the last can often be forgotten. 'And you shall glorify
me.' This, however, is the privilege Yahweh's servants
should be enjoying.

It may surprise us that the God who is so critical of
Israel's worship (vv. 8-13) should turn round, as it were,
and extend such a privilege to them. He is clearly a judge
but a gracious judge. I like the story I read in a local
newspaper in June, 2000. It told of a court in Fairfax

---

8   'Pull out' (*halas.*) is usually 'rescue' or 'deliver' in most
translations. I've kept a more literal sense—cf. Lev. 14:40, 43,
where contaminated stones are pulled out or torn out of a house; so
Yahweh pulls His servants out of their distresses. Cf. TWOT, 1:292.

County, Virginia, Judge Donald McDonough presiding. A raft of landlord-tenant disputes, one after another, something like 150 of them. But at 10 o'clock one Friday morning, the judge's rapid-fire system took a pause. There was something about the middle-aged deaf couple standing there, facing eviction for falling $250 behind in their rent. The landlord insisted on a judgment against them. McDonough abruptly left the bench, returned a minute later with two crisp $100 bills and a $50 in his hands, leaned over the bench, handed the bills to the landlord's baffled attorney, and said, 'Consider it paid.' Who would have thought! Help from a judge. But that's what we have in Psalm 50: Yahweh the judge who critiques His people's foolish worship also provides them with the formula for faithful worship.

In the third section, God speaks to another contingent of the 'covenant people' and we hear **the God who condemns** (vv. 16-22). We can track our way through this section if we note the matters of identity (v. 16a), hypocrisy (vv. 16b-20), fallacy (v. 21), and urgency (v. 22).

'But to the wicked God says' (v. 16a). 'Wicked' here is singular and God's address continues in the second person singular down through verse 21. In verse 22, the verb ('Get the point') is plural as well as the address ('forgetters of God'). The singular is used in verses 16-21, but verse 22 makes clear that the Lord addresses a contingent of folks. But who are the wicked? Clearly, in the context of the psalm, they are part of the 'covenant ones' (v. 5). The wicked are within the covenant people; they are not pagans but Israelites. And here they are among God's people, mouthing allegiance to God's covenant and reciting His commandments (v. 16).

So Yahweh charges them with hypocrisy, a hypocrisy in attitude (vv. 16b-17) and in action (vv. 18-20). They don't give a rip about Yahweh's Word or requirements (v. 17) and that attitude is on display in their conduct (vv. 18-20), as they cozy up to eighth-commandment-breakers (v. 18a), hob-nob with seventh-commandment-breakers (v. 18b), and become ninth-commandment-breakers as they mouth deceit and bring false charges even against ones in their own families (vv. 19-20). They recite the Apostles' Creed and live like the mafia.

In all this, the wicked man has committed a horrible error. 'These things you have done,' Yahweh says, 'and I kept quiet.' Because of that divine 'silence,' 'you thought I was just like yourself' (v. 21a). There was no immediate judgment, no obvious recompence, no calamitous punishment—hence the wicked infer the indifference of God (Eccles. 8:11; cf. 2 Pet. 3:3-4). 'You thought I was just like yourself.' There is the fallacy in their thinking.

False thinking can set one up for a devastating blow. Barbara Tuchman tells how the first decade of the twentieth century closed with Europe at ease. Nineteen-ten was peaceful and prosperous, and it was about then that a new book, *The Great Illusion* by Norman Angell, had been published. The volume proved that war 'had become vain.' Angell supported his thesis by examples and argument, showing that, given the financial and economic inter-locking of nations, war's winners would suffer as much as its losers. War had become unprofitable. 'Therefore no nation would be so foolish as to start one.' The volume gathered a cult-like following, study groups galore. That there would be, could be, war was the great illusion. After all, it made no sense.[9] But come 1914, *The Great Illusion* proved to be a great illusion. It's shattering to see one's axioms have been asinine.

No, God will not always keep silent (see v. 3a). That's why He delivers His 'bare knuckles' threat:

> Get the point, you forgetters of God,
> lest I tear you apart
>   and there's no one to deliver (v. 22).

That's a terribly harsh word—it's meant to be. But if one has ears to hear, one can detect a tad of invitation in it. There seems to be a hint that there might be a possibility for repentance.

And we need to watch our own thinking at this point. So easy for Christians to come up with nonsense here, like: That was the Old Testament (said with a note of disparagement) and we all know that Israel was a 'mixed bag' of believers and hypocrites (the implication being that somehow things are different with us). But Jesus assumed the situation would be similar among His disciples—there would be those who fervently dropped His name ('Lord, Lord') and preached and cast out demons and carried out successful ministries who would yet have to hear His 'I never knew you' (Matt. 7:21-23).

Yahweh's particular address to the wicked concludes at the end of verse 22. Verse 23 is a summary-piece for the whole psalm. The translation of this verse is a bit difficult, but it seems plain enough that it is a word of assurance to those who practice verses 14-15, who so worship and

---

9   Barbara Tuchman, *The Guns of August* (New York: Bonanza Books, 1982), pp. 9-10.

'set (their) way.' When Yahweh says, 'I will show him the salvation of God,' we can safely assume that it includes those times of deliverance in 'the day of trouble' noted in verse 15. And yet, it seems fuller than that: 'he shall see God's salvation, both in the narrower sense of daily interpositions for deliverance, and in the wider of a full and final rescue from all evil and endowment with all good.'[10] There's no reason an Old Testament text can't talk like that.

---

10   Alexander Maclaren, *The Psalms*, 3 vols. (reprint ed., Minneapolis: Klock & Klock, 1981), 2:124.

Psalm 51

To the music leader. A psalm of David, when Nathan the prophet went in to him after he had had relations with Bathsheba.

(1) Show grace to me, O God,
    in line with your faithful love,
    in line with your massive compassions
  wipe out my rebellions.

(2) Wash me completely from my iniquity,
  and cleanse me from my sin;

(3) for I know my rebellions
  and my sin (is) constantly in front of me.

(4) Against you, you alone, I have sinned,
  and I have done what is evil in your eyes,
    so that you might be in the right when you speak
    and in the clear when you judge.

(5) Indeed, I was born in iniquity;
  I was a sinner when my mother conceived me.

(6) Indeed, you have desired truth in the inward parts,
  and in the hidden place you will make me know wisdom.

(7) You will de-sin me with hyssop
    and I will be clean;
  you will wash me,
    and I will be whiter than snow.

(8) You will make me hear joy and gladness
    —the bones you have crushed will shout for joy.

(9) Hide your face from my sins
and wipe out my iniquities.

(10) Create for me a clean heart, O God,
and renew a steadfast spirit within me.

(11) Don't cast me away from your presence,
and don't take your holy Spirit from me.

(12) Bring back to me the joy of your salvation
and support me with a willing spirit.

(13) I will teach rebels your ways
and sinners will return to you.

(14) Deliver me from bloodguilt, O God,
   God of my salvation
   —my tongue will ring with joy over your righteousness.

(15) Lord, you will open my lips,
and my mouth will declare your praise.

(16) For you will not be pleased with a sacrifice
   —or I would give it;
   you will not accept a burnt-offering.

(17) My sacrifice, O God, is a broken spirit,
a heart broken and crushed, O God, you will never despise.

(18) Do good in your favor to Zion,
may you build the walls of Jerusalem.

(19) Then you can be pleased with righteous sacrifices,
   a burnt-offering, a whole burnt-offering;
   then they will offer up bulls on your altar.

13

CRUSHED HEART

Someone has said that the church is the only place where people confess sins. Probably so. They don't confess sins in the United States Senate, nor in the Rotary Club or at the stock market or in school board meetings or at conventions of professors of sociology. You get the picture. Only in church. Maybe. Why 'maybe'? Because sometimes, in some churches, one can be hard put to find prayer at all, let alone confession of sin. 'Evangelical' churches are no exception. One may hear a quick prayer at the first of the service and one at the end (been there, heard this). But there are some who make room for a prayer of confession (led by the minister or an elder, or else said in unison). One of my pastor friends once waxed ecstatic over the prayer of confession in worship, because, as he exclaimed, it means 'We get to repent!'

That is welcome news. In fact, repentance is one evidence that the Spirit of God has worked a saving change in us. Check out Ezekiel 36:22-32, and note especially verse 31: 'Then you will remember your evil ways, and your deeds that were not good; *and you will loathe yourselves for your iniquities and your abominable deeds*' (RSV; emphasis mine). If you note the preceding context, it is clear that this self-loathing is the *evidence* of a new heart and a new spirit. (Don't worry about what your psycho-therapist may tell you about your delicate self-image.) Indeed, Jonathan Edwards held that there were certain evidences missing in those who have no true grace, one of which was an abiding sense of sin.[1] So repentance should be one of our finest exercises, as it is for David in this psalm.

Psalm 51 is a bit dangerous for us, however. You look at the superscription that recalls 2 Samuel 11-12, and you may subtly look down on David. Well, because he, for example, committed adultery and you haven't...overtly... yet. Another pastor friend of mine once alluded to Corrie Ten Boom and confessed, 'She has more spirituality in her little finger than I have in my whole body.' That's the way we should think about David here, for he is grand in his repentance, far grander than any proud Presbyterians (or other 'franchises') in their rectitude.

The psalm breaks down into four sections: (1) the heading, (2) verses 1-9, (3) verses 10-17, then (4) the tailpiece, verses 18-19. The two major sections begin and end on similar notes. Verses 1-9 begin with iniquity and sin (vv. 1-2) and come back to iniquities and sins (v. 9). Verses 10-17 begin with 'heart' and 'spirit' (v. 10) and close out with 'spirit' and 'heart' (v. 17). Let's work

---

1   Iain H. Murray, *Jonathan Edwards* (Edinburgh: Banner of Truth, 1987), pp. 258-59.

our way through the psalm, keeping our eyes on the main foci.

First, David speaks of **the God I seek**. We see this in the heading and in verses 1-2. He seeks grace and the God of grace. His very first words are 'Show grace to me, O God.'[2] This plea sort of reverses our attention to the heading where we've already seen something of the scheme of grace. We read: 'when Nathan the prophet went in to him.' But why did Nathan go to him? 'And Yahweh sent Nathan to David' (2 Sam. 12:1). He sent Nathan to flush David out and expose his guilt. This is the hard and severe work of grace which is nevertheless gracious.

And so David expresses his need of grace:

> Wipe out my rebellions,
> Wash me completely from my iniquity,
> and cleanse me from my sin (vv. 1b-2).

Here he provides us with a pile of sin-words. *Pesha'* is more than 'transgression,' more like revolt or rebellion. It's what David did when he despised the Word of Yahweh, indeed, despised Yahweh (2 Sam. 12:9, 10). 'Iniquity' (*'awon*) has the idea of perversity or twistedness. I can't help but think of what John Blanchard once wrote about George Wald. Wald won the Nobel Prize for physiology in 1967. Blanchard quotes Wald:

> When it comes to the origin of life on earth, there are only two possibilities: creation or spontaneous generation. Spontaneous generation was disproved 100 years ago, but that leads us to only one other conclusion:

---

2   'Have mercy' is the traditional translation, but the very root (Heb. *ḥnn*) carries the idea of 'show grace.'

that of supernatural creation. *We cannot accept that . . .*
therefore *we choose to believe the impossible* that life arose
spontaneously by chance.[3]

That is what we call blind faith; it's also perversity,
twistedness, the idea behind 'iniquity.' Then David
mentioned 'sin' (*ḥatta't*), a term sometimes associated
with 'missing the mark,' falling short, like a shot in
basketball that doesn't even reach the rim.

But even with this complex of guilt, David has
hope in grace. But can you believe his audacity? 'Wipe
out ... wash ... cleanse.' He wants God to delete the
record and purge the defilement. Wherever did he get
such an idea? How can he even dream of such a possibility?
Do you go into the bank that holds your mortgage and ask
the manager to cancel your debt?

Verse 1, of course, holds the answer:

Show grace to me, O God,
> *in line with your faithful love,*
> *in line with your massive compassions*
wipe out my rebellions (emphasis mine).

His petition rests on the kind of God he has; he has hope
because of the character of God, a God of *ḥesed* (faithful
love) and massive compassions.

I know I've alluded to it before, but when I was a lad
there was a rigid rule enforced in our home. No whistling
in the house. If myself or one of my brothers let go with
a bit of lyrical air, and, assuming my father was within
earshot, we would hear an emphatic, no-nonsense decree

---

3   John Blanchard, *Is God Past His Sell-by Date?* (Darlington: Evangelical Press, 2002), p. 93. Emphasis in original.

repeated: 'No whistling in the house.' As one grows and matures and even reaches adulthood, one begins to wonder about the rationale behind the command. Did it disturb my father's study? Did his father impose such nonsense on him? I even asked my mother—one would think she would be in on the secret. She was non-plussed; she had no idea why my father inflicted such a statute. That was just the way he was. And because he was that way, we regulated our conduct accordingly. Now in principle, though positively, that's why David makes the petitions he does. Surely he can't explain *why* Yahweh exercises ḥesed or overflowing compassions. But that's just the way He is. And because He is that kind of God, David can make 'absurd' requests like rebellions being wiped out and getting cleansed from iniquity. If you lay hold of the character of God, it leads you to ask wild things, like 'wipe out my rebellions.'

The sense we should get from the text is that this is almost too much to hope for. It's something like the story Clarence Macartney once told. In the laboratory of the renowned chemist Faraday, a workman accidentally dropped a very costly silver cup into a tank of strong acid. He and other workers helplessly watched the hasty disintegration of the cup. But Faraday, having seen what had occurred, poured a chemical into the tank. The silver was precipitated to the bottom and recovered, and the shapeless mass was sent off to the silversmith to be refashioned as it once had been. Almost too much to hope for, like cleansing from sin.

Secondly, David speaks of **the sin I know** (vv. 3-9). Here David supports his plea for cleansing (vv. 1-2) with the admission that he is acutely conscious of his guilt.

'For **I** [emphatic] know my rebellions.' And he realizes that his sin has been supremely against Yahweh Himself. Of course, if there is no consciousness of sin (vv. 3-4), there will hardly be petitions for cleansing (vv. 1-2). It is quite easy to be blind in such matters. Irvin McDowell was the first general to lead Union forces in the American Civil War. He was six feet tall, heavy-set, and generally congenial. He was dead set against the use of alcohol. But some were appalled over his humongous appetite. One onlooker was shocked as he watched McDowell, after having a full meal, polish off a whole watermelon for dessert and dub it 'monstrous fine.' He was virtuous over alcohol but utterly blind to gluttony. That's the way we often are. It takes light from above to say, 'I know my rebellions.' David himself didn't see his until Nathan tricked him with his poor-man's-lamb routine (see 2 Sam. 12:1-7a).

But David not only speaks of the consciousness of his sin but of the aggravation of his sin:

> Indeed, I was born in iniquity;
> I was a sinner when my mother conceived me (v. 5).

He isn't saying that there was something shady or immoral about his birth, neither is he trying to excuse his sin, as if to say, 'That's just the way I am—I can't help it.' Rather he is saying that he has been evil right from the start, not, again, to excuse his sin but to aggravate it, almost as if to say, 'No surprise there, for I am just like that.' He does not *excuse* his sin in verse 5, he *explains* it.

Let's pause a moment. It's because people in general, and politicians and social reformers in particular, ignore this matter of sinful human nature that their idealistic dreams and schemes litter the path of history with their shattered pieces. Barbara Tuchman wrote *The Guns of August* about the First World War. On the frontispiece of that book she included a quote from Marechal de Saxe: 'The human heart is the starting point of all matters pertaining to war.' Charles Colson wrote of this depravity of human nature in his *Kingdoms in Conflict*. He tells of Armando Valladares, a Cuban poet who spoke out against Castro's communism and was locked up in the gross confines of a Cuban prison for twenty-two years. Sadistic guards gave him showers of human urine and excrement. During an escape attempt he broke three bones in his leg. The escapees were captured, brought back to the cell and stripped. The guards used thick, twisted electric cables and truncheons to beat him. In a whirl of vertigo, he felt like he was being branded with a red-hot branding iron, but then, he says, he suddenly experienced the 'most intense, unbearable, and brutal pain of my life'—one of the guards jumped with all his weight on his broken leg. Colson then comments:

> One cannot read this and explain the torture, the sadism, and the evil only in terms of godless political systems. The problem is human nature. The only progress between Cain and the Communist jailers of Armando Valladares has been the technological sophistication of cruelty.[4]

So why are we surprised when an Israelite king shacks up with another man's wife and then arranges the demise of her husband? Why are we surprised that helpless

---

4   Charles Colson, *Kingdoms in Conflict* (Grand Rapids: Morrow/ Zondervan, 1987), p. 77.

Nigerian Christians are wantonly gunned down by Islamic terrorists? Why are we shocked at the barrage of shootings at malls and schools and celebrations that clutter our news? I have often said that I've been glad to have members of the Highway Patrol or local police in our congregations— one doesn't have to convince *them* of the depravity of human nature. If you don't get this right (what Reformed theologians call total depravity), your view of the world and culture will always be skewed and you will set yourself up for ongoing disappointment and disillusionment.

As David goes on praying, he speaks of *hope in the face of sin* (vv. 6-8). Already he has a degree of assurance. Not all will take these verses this way, so we need to get a bit pedantic and explain. Note the translation I have given:

> (6) Indeed, you have desired truth in the inward parts,
> and in the hidden place you will make me know
> wisdom.

> (7) You will de-sin me with hyssop
> and I will be clean;
> you will wash me,
> and I will be whiter than snow.

> (8) You will make me hear joy and gladness
> —the bones you have crushed will shout for joy.

Compare this with other translations (e.g., ESV, NASB, NIV). Usually, the verbs are taken as imperatives, making requests. But they are more likely what in English we'd call indicatives, making statements or giving assurances. The verb forms in question are Hebrew 'imperfects.' Sometimes they can be used as imperatives or for making requests, but if that had been the intent, straight imperatives could have been used as in verses 1-2 and 9.

Instead, they should be taken as statements—and so David here expresses his hope even in the face of his sin.[5]

So then, here David speaks of what God will give him. He specifies:

> The discernment you will give, 6b
> The defilement you will cleanse, 7[6]
> The delight you will restore, 8

Even in repentance for sin of the deepest dye, David is not bereft of some firm assurances. He is essentially saying to the Lord: 'What I need you will give.'

Now, for a moment, let's jump out of verses 3-9, for a quick look at verse 14, where we see the horror of David's sin. If there are assurances (vv. 6-8), there is also the terror of sin: 'Deliver me from bloodguilt, O God.' 'Bloodguilt' is, literally, 'bloods.' He means the bloodshed in bringing about Uriah's death (2 Sam. 11:6-25). How can one be delivered from *that*? This seems like an outburst that erupts in the middle of David's describing how he desires to be restored (vv. 10-15). Bloodguilt. David cannot forget Uriah's murder. David remembers the crocodile tears behind Uriah's casket, the full military honors he ordered for Uriah's funeral, the pious drivel at the press conference about Yahweh taking 'one of our most noble warriors' from us, the hawkish words he had uttered at the grave-side service about the 'Ammonite killers' and

---

5 I am no 'lone ranger' in taking this position. Alexander, Perowne, Kirkpatrick, and Kidner all take this view. Those interested can check their commentaries.

6 'You will de-sin me with hyssop' likely has an eye on Lev. 14:4ff. Hyssop was the herb used in sprinkling the cleansing solution on a leper when he was 'cleansed.'

the 'moral outrage' he felt. Yet David can still see Uriah's blood dripping in his dreams.

What then can we say about this whole 'the sin I know' section? Perhaps the best word can come from a Scottish lady. When Alexander Whyte (1836–1921), the renowned Scottish preacher, was a lad, his arm got caught in a threshing machine and everyone thought he would lose it. Everyone, except a neighbor who, in a down-home way, was skilled in such matters. She wouldn't let them take the boy to the hospital for surgery. The pain became worse, and Whyte's mother sent for the neighbor woman again. She looked over the boy and the injury again and said: 'I like the pain. I like the pain.' She was spot on. The arm healed. The pain was apparently the first step toward recovery.[7] Perhaps that's how we should look at it: we like the pain because it's the first step in giving place to the faithfulness of God (1 John 1:9).

Thirdly, David speaks of **the restoration I need** (vv. 10-15). This restoration involves four foci, the first being *a divine work*:

> Create for me a clean heart, O God,
> and renew a steadfast spirit within me (v. 10).

As is often said, the verb *bara'* ('create') in its main stem always refers to divine activity and so to what lies beyond the sphere of human ability.[8] He wants an internal purging that can only be God's gift—and an ongoing stability ('a steadfast spirit') that does not fall away from the path of fidelity.

This restoration also seems to involve *a genuine fear*: 'Don't cast me away from your presence, and don't take your

---

7   Warren W. Wiersbe, *Living with the Giants* (Grand Rapids: Baker, 1993), p. 125.
8   TWOT, 1:127.

holy Spirit from me' (v. 11). Is David not here pleading that God would not give him the 'Saul treatment'? After Saul's repeated rebellions, when David had been anointed king and the Spirit of Yahweh had 'rushed upon him' (1 Sam. 16:13), we read that the Spirit of Yahweh 'departed from Saul and a distressing spirit from Yahweh terrified him' (1 Sam. 16:14). Once more we read that Yahweh 'had departed from Saul' (1 Sam. 18:12). There is nothing so terrifying as forfeiting the friendship of God (cf. Ps. 30:7). My hunch is that the memory of Saul's disaster comes fresh to David's mind—and he prays he will be spared from it. Clearly David's restoration has begun, for if this is his fear, it is clearly a *faithful* fear.

David also needs *a positive delight*: 'bring back to me the joy of your salvation (v. 12a). As some have said, he does not ask that salvation be restored but the joy of it. And then another part of his restoration involved *an effective testimony* (vv. 13, 15). After confession and forgiveness, David vows to 'teach rebels your ways' in order, one assumes, to recover them. Allen Ross asserts that David has something particular in mind here when he mention's God's 'ways':

> The ways of the LORD in this psalm must have to do with forgiveness, for if he was to teach them about God's punishment for sin or about God's holiness he did not need forgiveness to do that. In this context, the 'ways' must refer to the divine attributes of God's grace, loyal love, and abundant mercy, which bring forgiveness and renewal. So once forgiven, the psalmist vows to teach other sinners how to find forgiveness—and in the writing of this psalm he has done that for centuries.[9]

---

9   Allen Ross, *A Commentary on the Psalm*, 3 vols. (Grand Rapids: Kregel, 2013), 2:196.

So David looks for a testimony of grace (v. 13) and also of praise (v. 15).

David then looks beyond forgiveness to restoration, a restoration that craves steadfastness and communion and joy and testimony.

Perhaps something of a 'political' analogy will be useful here. General Dwight Eisenhower came back as a military hero from World War II and was then a shoo-in for a two-term presidency in the USA. But being such a VIP for years meant he became used to VIP treatment, which meant that 'little people' around him tended to all the details. While 'Ike' was president he even had his personal valet dress him. John Moaney would put on Eisenhower's watch while the president held out his wrist and would pull up his boss's boxer shorts! But this sort of pampering became problematical after Ike left the White House. At that point, he was almost completely ignorant about how to pay for things at a department store, how to adjust a TV set, get past a toll booth on the highway, or even to dial a phone.[10] Eisenhower needed help to know how to go on after the presidency. And in verses 10-15, David is saying something similar: there are certain provisions he needs for living in post-forgiveness time.

Finally, David tells of **the worship I bring** (vv. 16-17).[11] He speaks first of the depth of his worship:

---

10   Cormac O'Brien, *Secret Lives of the U. S. Presidents* (Philadelphia: Quirk Books, 2004), p. 203.

11   Verses 18-19 seems like an addition to the psalm. I don't know when they were added, if they were. They could be David's own footnote, or they could have been appended by some Psalm editors later. If we take verse 19 seriously, then obviously the psalm, and especially verses 16-17, do not negate the proper function of the OT

For you will not be pleased with a sacrifice
—or I would give it;
you will not accept a burnt-offering.
My sacrifice, O God, is a broken spirit (vv. 16-17a).

David is not 'putting down' sacrifices or burnt-offerings. He is implying that God wouldn't be pleased with simply the external act of a sacrifice or burnt-offering. Rather, the Lord looks for something deeper: 'My sacrifice, O God, is a broken spirit' (v. 17a).[12] The text implies that what is required are not sacrifices or mere prayers of confession or liturgical gimmicks; there's an internal 'sacrifice' that must be in place. It goes without saying that such a text ought to put a pause on the flippant, rapid-fire, throw-away line at the end of some 'Christian' prayers—'and forgive us of our many, many sins, in Jesus' name, Amen.'

If my sacrifice is a 'broken spirit' (v. 17a), there's a certain assurance of *acceptance* I can have: 'a heart broken and crushed, O God, you will never despise' (v. 17b). And this simply drives us back to verse 1, where David has the gall to pray, 'Show grace to me, O God,' and where he lays his head down on the pillow of divine mercy. 'But there is forgiveness with you, that you may be feared' (Ps. 130:4).

How many of God's people have repented by, lived in, and reveled in Psalm 51 through the centuries. But I find

---

sacrificial system; yet the fact that verse 19 follows the psalm shows that the external offering of sacrifices must be done with an earnest and sincere disposition.

12   Most versions and translations render 17a, 'The sacrifices of God are ....' But a mere change of vowels (not of the original text) on the first word gives the rendering 'My sacrifice'; cf. TEV, JB, NEB, NRSV mg.

especially moving a tribute Professor John Murray gave regarding his father. It was early January 1942 when Prof. Murray, who was in Philadelphia, heard that his father had died in Scotland. Murray wrote of the sad news to his pastor, telling him how his father had witnessed to the Lord to the ripe age of ninety. Then his letter goes on:

> His interest was lively and his faculties unimpaired, until, just a few weeks ago, his interest in things of this world seemed largely to disappear. In the last letter I had from my sister she told me that, for the two days preceding, he was in the 51st psalm and repeated it again and again from the beginning to the end in Gaelic, his mother tongue, of course.[13]

What better words can you have on your tongue until the moment when your tongue can no longer say, 'A heart broken and crushed, O God, you will never despise'?

---

13   Iain H. Murray, 'Life of John Murray,' in *Collected Writings of John Murray*, vol. 3 (Edinburgh: Banner of Truth, 1982), p. 82.

Christian Focus Publications

Our mission statement –

STAYING FAITHFUL
In dependence upon God we seek to impact the world through literature faithful to His infallible Word, the Bible. Our aim is to ensure that the Lord Jesus Christ is presented as the only hope to obtain forgiveness of sin, live a useful life and look forward to heaven with Him.

Our books are published in four imprints:

CHRISTIAN FOCUS

Popular works including biographies, commentaries, basic doctrine and Christian living.

CHRISTIAN HERITAGE

Books representing some of the best material from the rich heritage of the church.

MENTOR

Books written at a level suitable for Bible College and seminary students, pastors, and other serious readers. The imprint includes commentaries, doctrinal studies, examination of current issues and church history.

CF4•K

Children's books for quality Bible teaching and for all age groups: Sunday school curriculum, puzzle and activity books; personal and family devotional titles, biographies and inspirational stories – because you are never too young to know Jesus!

Christian Focus Publications Ltd,
Geanies House, Fearn, Ross-shire,
IV20 1TW, Scotland, United Kingdom.
www.christianfocus.com
blog.christianfocus.com